THE
EVERYTHING®
BIG BOOK OF EASY
LARGE-PRINT CROSSWORDS

Dear Reader,

I know a secret about crossword puzzles: They can be a lot of fun, even if you are not an expert solver. I think the problem with so many crossword puzzles is that they are really difficult. The solving stops long before the grid is filled, and that is no fun! These puzzles are different. You will probably know some, but not all, of the answers the first time you go through a puzzle's clues. Those answers will give you the crossing letters to help you solve more of the puzzle. And that is when the fun really begins, as you are able to fill in more and more of the grid. It's very satisfying!

Another nice thing about these puzzles is that they're large. With bigger text, the clues are easier to read. With bigger grids, the answers are easier to write. It makes the solving experience much more pleasant.

You're now in on my secret. I think you are going to have a fun and rewarding time solving these puzzles!

Charles Timmerman

Welcome to the Everything® Series!

These handy, accessible books give you all you need to tackle a difficult project, gain a new hobby, comprehend a fascinating topic, prepare for an exam, or even brush up on something you learned back in school but have since forgotten.

You can choose to read an Everything® book from cover to cover or just pick out the information you want from our four useful boxes: Questions, Facts, Alerts, and Essentials. We give you everything you need to know on the subject, but throw in a lot of fun stuff along the way too.

We now have more than 600 Everything® books in print, spanning such wide-ranging categories as cooking, health, parenting, personal finance, wedding planning, word puzzles, and so much more. When you're done reading them all, you can finally say you know Everything®!

PUBLISHER Karen Cooper
MANAGING EDITOR Lisa Laing
COPY CHIEF Casey Ebert
PRODUCTION EDITOR Jo-Anne Duhamel
EVERYTHING® SERIES COVER DESIGNER Erin Alexander
COVER DESIGNER Alaya Howard

THE EVERYTHING®

BIG BOOK

of **EASY**

LARGE-PRINT

CROSSWORDS

125+

**EASY CROSSWORD PUZZLES
IN EASY-TO-READ PRINT!**

Charles Timmerman
Founder of Funster.com

Adams Media
New York   London   Toronto   Sydney   New Delhi

Dedicated to Suzanne, Calla, and Meryl

Aadamsmedia

Adams Media
An Imprint of Simon & Schuster, Inc.
100 Technology Center Drive
Stoughton, Massachusetts 02072

An Everything® Series Book.
Everything® and everything.com® are registered trademarks of Simon & Schuster, Inc.

First Adams Media trade paperback edition June 2021

ADAMS MEDIA and colophon are trademarks of Simon & Schuster.

For information about special discounts for bulk purchases, please contact Simon & Schuster Special Sales at 1-866-506-1949 or business@simonandschuster.com.

The Simon & Schuster Speakers Bureau can bring authors to your live event. For more information or to book an event contact the Simon & Schuster Speakers Bureau at 1-866-248-3049 or visit our website at www.simonspeakers.com.

Manufactured in the United States of America

10 9 8 7 6 5

ISBN 978-1-5072-1647-7

Acknowledgments

I would like to thank each and every one of the more than half million people who have visited my website, Funster.com, to play word games and puzzles. You have shown me how much fun puzzles can be and how addictive they can become!

It is a pleasure to acknowledge the folks at Adams Media who made this book possible. I particularly want to thank my editor, Lisa Laing, for so skillfully managing the many projects we have worked on together.

Contents

Introduction

What do Rosa Parks, Richard Nixon, Jesse Owens, and crossword puzzles have in common? They were all born in the year 1913. In that year, a journalist named Arthur Wynne published a "word-cross puzzle" in the *New York World*'s Sunday newspaper. Though it was diamond-shaped, it had all of the features of the crossword puzzles that we know and love today. The name evolved into *crossword* as the paper continued to publish the popular word puzzles.

It wasn't until 1924 that the first book of crossword puzzles was published. That was when the crossword craze really began. It joined other fads of the Roaring Twenties like goldfish swallowing, flagpole sitting, yo-yos, and pogo sticks. Of course, not all of these fads survived (perhaps fortunately).

Besides crossword puzzles, some really beautiful things came out of the 1920s. In music, jazz surged in popularity and George Gershwin's *Rhapsody in Blue* was performed for the first time. In literature, F. Scott Fitzgerald published some of his most enduring novels, including *The Great Gatsby*.

In design, it was the beginning of art deco. That's how the world was shifting when crossword puzzles came of age.

Crossword puzzles became popular closer to a time when entertainment required *active* participation. In those days, people actually played sports rather than watched them, told each other stories rather than turning on the TV, and even sang songs rather than streaming them. Like entertainment of yesteryear, crossword puzzles require your active participation. And this is a refreshing change for those of us who still enjoy a mental workout.

Today, nearly every major newspaper runs a crossword puzzle. Entire sections of bookstores are devoted to crossword puzzle books. (Thanks for choosing this one!) Indeed, crosswords are probably the most common word puzzle in the world.

Why do crossword puzzles continue to be so popular? Only you can answer that question, since there are as many reasons to work a crossword puzzle as there are solvers. But perhaps it has something to do with the convenient marriage of fun and learning that crossword puzzles offer.

Puzzles

ACROSS

1. Montgomery is its cap.
4. Lower in public estimation
9. "Give ___ little time"
12. Hawaiian neckwear
13. Parts to play
14. End of many URLs
15. Guy's mate
16. Pepsi and RC
17. Letter after *zeta*
18. Sports venues
20. Group of buffalo
22. Signed off
23. ___ Stone (hieroglyphics key)
26. Activist Chavez
28. Legendary pitcher Dizzy
29. Bird's bill
32. Aliens, for short
33. Church service
34. Pint, inch, or second
35. Former Attorney General Edwin
37. Big steps
39. Throws
43. Church benches
44. Call it a day
45. Sis's sibling
47. Patriot Allen
49. Scottish denial
50. Rower's blade
51. Africa's Sierra ___
52. Good Samaritan's offering
53. ___ Offensive (Vietnam War event)
54. Horses' gaits
55. ___ and outs (intricacies)

DOWN

1. Seaweed
2. Acquire knowledge
3. Troubled
4. Pinball palace
5. Sounds of disapproval
6. Pledge of Allegiance ending
7. Fish that swims upright
8. Letters before tees
9. Lemonade alternative
10. Little tyke
11. Simon & Garfunkel's "I ___ Rock"
19. Suit accessory
21. Beef, e.g.
23. Lenders' charges
24. Prof's aides, briefly
25. Reply to a ques.
27. College half-year
29. School transportation
30. Suffix with differ
31. Control tower location
36. Behind the ___
38. Lived (in)
40. Mideast peninsula
41. Prepare for a bout

Puzzle 1

42. Watermelon throwaways
44. Long, angry complaint
45. Droid
46. Filmdom's *Norma* ___
48. "Yoo-___!"

Solution on Page 272

ACROSS

1. Solvers' shouts
5. Boston ___ Orchestra
9. Part of WWW
12. Debussy's "Clair de ___"
13. "Put a sock ___!"
14. Conscious self, to Freud
15. Costing nothing
16. Chancellor von Bismarck
17. Trail the pack
18. Achieve
20. Gives in
22. Doggie doc
24. Subway unit
25. "___ tree falls…"
28. "___-haw!" (rodeo cry)
29. Funnyman Foxx
32. Recycling containers
34. Sought political office
36. ___-mutuel (form of betting)
37. Breakfast, lunch, or dinner
38. Cartoon frame
40. Dance club VIPs
41. ___-de-sac (blind alley)
43. Med. plan
44. Unconcerned with right and wrong
47. Overabundance
52. Something confessed in a confessional
53. Clothing store department

55. "___ Have to Do Is Dream"
56. Neither Rep. nor Dem.
57. Prefix with disestablishmentarianism
58. "Read 'em and ___!"
59. Mortgage org.
60. Stadium cheers
61. Makes clothes

DOWN

1. ___ Romeo
2. William of *Broadcast News*
3. Operating without ___ (taking risks)
4. "I ___ bad moon rising"
5. Conestoga rider
6. Niagara Falls's prov.
7. Feel sorry for
8. Stiff-upper-lip type
9. Bookish
10. Old-time exclamation
11. Sources of peat
19. Yale's league
21. Wyatt at the O.K. Corral
23. Instruct
25. Big name in early PCs
26. "Fee, ___, foe, fum"
27. Large snake
30. Julius Erving's nickname
31. Speak ill of, in slang
33. Nasty remark

35. Archenemy

39. Bagel topper

42. Tennessee senator Alexander

44. "Like, no way!"

45. Ho Chi ___ City

46. Horne or Olin

48. Crow calls

49. "Waiting for the Robert ___"

50. Dispatched, as a dragon

51. Drinks slowly

54. To the ___ power

Solution on Page 272

ACROSS

1. Top card in a royal flush
4. "Killer" PC program
7. As neat as ___
11. Espionage gp.
12. *Dragon's* ___ (early video game)
14. Author Ephron
15. Letters on a telephone bill
16. Fortune-teller's start
17. Aussie's greeting
18. Take offense at
20. "One": Fr.
22. Really small
23. Deli meat
27. Evaluate
30. Tooth covering
31. Trigger's rider
32. Jim and Tammy's old club
33. Knights' weapons
37. Auntie Em's home
40. Ultimatum words
41. Timetable abbr.
42. "Solve for x" subj.
43. Responds
47. Wire diameter units
50. McGregor of *Angels & Demons*
52. Be ill
53. Quickly: abbr.
54. Prefix with tiller
55. Grazing place
56. Emulates Eminem
57. Soaked
58. Crow's call

DOWN

1. Rent-___ (airport service)
2. Issue a ticket to
3. Stops fasting
4. Flared skirts
5. Puts in the scrapbook
6. Dessert often served à la mode
7. Actress Lansbury
8. Pea holder
9. Savings plan, for short
10. Aye canceler
13. Put into service again
19. Ram's ma'am
21. Indian flatbread
24. Concert equipment
25. Prefix with morphosis
26. Miseries
27. Guthrie of folk
28. Rise sky-high
29. "Auld Lang ___"
34. Necklace fasteners
35. Course for new immigrants: abbr.
36. "Like a Rock" singer Bob
37. Activity with chops and kicks
38. "We ___ amused"
39. Gun grp.

44. Course after trig
45. "___ Yellow Ribbon Round the Ole Oak Tree"
46. Cole ___ (side dish)
47. Tarnish
48. "It ___ far far better thing…"
49. Drink like a dog

51. "Unbelievable!"

Solution on Page 272

ACROSS

1. ___ Raton, Fla.
5. Teen-___
9. Coffee holder
12. Iridescent gem
13. Skin opening
14. One ___ kind
15. Vegetable soup bean
16. Fall faller
17. US currency
18. TV chef Paula
19. Start of some aircraft carriers
20. Monster's loch
21. 1040 org.
23. Large coffee vessel
25. ___ Apso (dog breed)
28. Closely cropped style
32. Kind of poodle
33. West Pointer, e.g.
35. Wire service inits.
36. Heartfelt
38. Urban's opposite
40. Stars and Stripes land
41. Fireplace fuel
42. Palm tree fruit
45. Org. with merit badges
47. Like arson evidence
51. Baseball hitting stat
52. Fixes a squeak
53. College sports org.
54. "It's a mouse!"
55. Howls at the moon
56. Turkey meat choice
57. Opus ___ (*The Da Vinci Code* group)
58. Not ___ many words
59. Insects in colonies

DOWN

1. Not timid
2. Andy Taylor's TV son
3. "And it ___ to pass…"
4. Grammy winner Morissette
5. Great grade
6. Travels
7. Deletion
8. Boxing official
9. Pie à la ___
10. Roswell sightings
11. Guys' mates
20. SSE's opposite
22. Indy 500 and others
24. Fashionably outdated
25. Mil. officers
26. ___ polloi (commoners)
27. *The Fountainhead* writer Rand
28. B–F connection
29. Junkyard dog
30. ___ tree (cornered)
31. "Open ___ midnight"

34. Asia's ___ Peninsula

37. Billiard stick

39. Where Idi Amin ruled

41. Cowboy's rope

42. ___ Scott Decision

43. Busy as ___

44. Disneyland's Enchanted ___ Room

46. Stone and Stallone

48. Read, as bar codes

49. Male deer

50. Tibetan beasts

52. ___-Wan Kenobi of Star Wars

Solution on Page 272

ACROSS

1. Hits head-on
5. Astern
8. Detective Charlie
12. Clarinet cousin
13. Greatly regret
14. Sacred
15. Dark and handsome companion
16. Looking at it one way
18. Brews, as tea
20. Computer program suffix
21. Quick refresher
24. Slangy assent
27. Poverty-stricken
30. "Catch ya later!"
31. "Oh, what's the ___?"
32. Between ports
34. Brain wave test, briefly
35. Seeing red
36. Students
38. School fundraising gp.
39. *Baywatch* event
40. Fond du ___, Wisconsin
42. Connected to the Internet
46. Repeated
50. Blizzard feature
51. College digs
52. Don Ho's plunker
53. ___ consequence (insignificant)
54. Quantities: abbr.
55. Wanna-___ (pretenders)
56. Cranny's companion

DOWN

1. Putrefies
2. Like ___ out of hell
3. Furry tunneler
4. Make a choice
5. Pupil of Plato
6. Amusement
7. Black or green drink
8. Cereal in party mix
9. Pollen gatherer
10. Pacino and Capone
11. Bill ___, TV's "Science Guy"
17. Calendar abbreviation
19. "___ Was a Rollin' Stone" (1972 hit)
22. Holders of glasses
23. Phone numbers usually in parentheses
25. Beholder
26. Cribbage markers
27. Landfill
28. "Time ___ a premium"
29. Imminent danger warning
33. Make ___ for it (flee)
37. South Africa's Mandela
39. Color TV pioneer
41. Octopod's octet

43. Knowledge, for short
44. Taboo, to a tot
45. Furry Star Wars creature
46. State east of Wash.
47. Actor Hanks
48. Place for a bath
49. ___ out (just manage)

Solution on Page 273

ACROSS

1. Philosopher's question
4. Card holder: abbr.
7. Walked back and forth
12. "The Tell-Tale Heart" author
13. ___-jongg (Chinese game)
14. Deadly virus
15. Buck toppers
17. Visitor from another planet
18. Boo-hoo
19. Knight's weapon
20. *The Devil Wears* ___
23. Candy in a collectible dispenser
24. Ullmann or Tyler
25. Lovett of country music
28. Place for a gutter
32. ET's ride
33. Blackmore's Lorna
35. Russian plane
36. Patch up
38. Moon goddess
39. Word with punching or sleeping
40. "Ugh!"
42. Train tracks
44. Less cooked
47. To the ___ (fully)
48. "Don't Cry for Me Argentina" musical
49. Announce
53. Feasts
54. ___Kosh B'Gosh
55. ___ down (massage)
56. Aromas
57. Hardship
58. Cold War spy org.

DOWN

1. New Deal org.
2. Abbr. before a judge's name
3. "Are we there ___?"
4. The ___ City (capital of the Land of Oz)
5. ___ a one
6. Videotape format
7. Norman Vincent ___
8. In flames
9. Nickel or dime
10. Power co. product
11. Copenhagen native
16. PC screen type
20. Jack Horner's find
21. In abundance
22. Door-to-door cosmetics seller
23. Actor Sean
26. The sunny side, in sunny-side up
27. Costello or Grant
29. Prefix with -valent
30. Small container for liquids
31. Incubator items
34. Swimmers' ailment

37. Calorie counter

41. Unrefined

43. Rock's ___ Rose

44. Go back to square one on

45. Like die-hard fans

46. Overindulger of the grape

47. "The Bible Tells ___"

49. Wall Street index, with "the"

50. Noah's construction

51. Floor covering

52. Recede, as the tide

Solution on Page 273

ACROSS

1. Airport screening org.
4. Legal org.
7. Mantra chants
10. Hither's opposite
11. Astonishes
13. Singer/actress Zadora
14. Postpone, with "off"
15. Basic belief
16. Prefix with angle or cycle
17. *Falstaff* and *Fidelio*
19. Tasty tidbit
21. Rudely abrupt
22. Have a debt
23. Largest Greek island
25. Illegal trader
29. Put 2 and 2 together
30. Road sign abbr.
31. Tree in many street names
32. Dangerous African flies
35. Madrid's country
37. Elevations: abbr.
38. Cooking grease
39. Give confidence to
42. Hawaiian greetings
45. Borrower's letters
46. "The ___ has landed"
48. "Evil Woman" rock group
49. Bambi's mother, e.g.
50. "Guilty" and "not guilty"
51. Follower of Mar.
52. Home for hogs
53. Do tailoring
54. Summer clock setting: abbr.

DOWN

1. Misprint
2. Minestrone, for example
3. Predate
4. "This is only ___"
5. Hot dog holder
6. Flowerlike sea creature
7. Elects (to)
8. "No time to wallow in the ___"
   (Doors lyric)
9. Jib or spinnaker
11. Fixed gaze
12. Packs away
18. Place to get stuck
20. Big outdoor gear retailer
23. Friskies eater
24. Travel rtes.
25. ___ *a Wonderful Life*
26. Fan of Jerry Garcia's band
27. Peyton Manning's brother
28. LBJ's successor
30. Closes again, as an envelope
33. Day of the wk.
34. Throat ailment
35. Red-tag events

36. Not con

38. TV show that had its Dey in court?

39. Lends a hand to

40. Chimney residue

41. Chop ___

43. Swiss range

44. Arrange from A to Z, say

47. "___ whillikers!"

Solution on Page 273

ACROSS

1. "It's ___-brainer!"
4. Respond to a stimulus
9. "__ Ho" (*Slumdog Millionaire* Oscar-winning song)
12. Fluorescent bulb alternative, for short
13. Concerning
14. Not safe, on the diamond
15. "Jimmy Crack Corn" sentiment
17. Web pop-ups, e.g.
18. Bon ___ (witticism)
19. Bucharest's land
21. *Let's Make ___*
23. Wynken and Blynken's partner
24. Gracefully slender
25. Spray can emission
29. "Honest" presidential nickname
30. Calif. clock setting
31. Greek T
32. Tel Aviv native
35. Keep from happening
37. Item under a blouse
38. Witherspoon of *Legally Blonde*
39. Droopy-eared hounds
43. ChapStick target
44. From ___ Z (totally)
45. Never-ending
49. Declare verboten
50. Eagle's claw
51. Train stop: abbr.
52. Taiwanese-born director Lee
53. Napped leather
54. Lao Tzu's ___ *Te Ching*

DOWN

1. He KO'd Foreman in '74
2. Homer's neighbor on *The Simpsons*
3. Mileage gauge
4. Baby's noisemaker
5. Exit-the-program key
6. At a distance
7. Small crown
8. Aftershock
9. Rivers of comedy
10. Auto with a four-ring logo
11. "___ Small World"
16. Trevor of *The Daily Show*
20. Uproar
21. Jai ___ (fast-moving sport)
22. Have ___ on (claim)
25. "Try ___ might…"
26. Least gradual
27. Dinghy propellers
28. Minstrel's instrument
30. Flat part of a chart line
33. Stomach muscles, informally
34. Puts up, as a tower
35. *What's My Line?* panelist Francis

24

36. Bridal wear

39. "Ali ___ and the Forty Thieves"

40. ___ impasse

41. Ballad, for example

42. Bargain event

46. Grass bought in rolls

47. Train stop: abbr.

48. ___ cone (summer treat)

Solution on Page 273

ACROSS

1. Moo ___ pork (Chinese dish)
4. Fizzling sound
8. Gee preceder
11. Shrill barks
13. Mechanic's grease job
14. Miracle-___
15. Nasdaq competitor
16. Fleischer and Onassis
17. ___-Xers (boomers' kids)
18. Mother Teresa, for one
20. Architect Frank ___ Wright
22. Hippie adornments
25. HS junior's exam
27. Thornton Wilder's ___ *Town*
28. Divide with a comb
30. Tenant's monthly check
34. Mork's home planet
35. More like a fox
37. Airport overseer: abbr.
38. Durante's famous feature
40. Johnny of Pirates of the Caribbean
41. Photo ___ (White House events)
42. Dec. 25
44. Female horses
46. Persona non ___
49. Food-additive letters
50. ___-pah band
51. Temperamental performer
54. ___ and flows
58. Duo
59. Open ___ of worms
60. Litigious sort
61. One way to get directions
62. Stubborn animal
63. ___ Friday's (restaurant chain)

DOWN

1. Roget entry: abbr.
2. Manger contents
3. Raises, as the ante
4. Architect's drawing
5. PETA peeve
6. G-man's org.
7. Electrical pioneer Nikola
8. Waffle brand
9. Glenn of the Eagles
10. Enamored (of)
12. Use Western Union, e.g.
19. Letter carriers' org.
21. Env. contents
22. Unexpected blessing
23. Continental money unit
24. Vessels like Noah's
25. Uses a lever
26. Big first for a baby
29. Alan of *The Four Seasons*
31. Get an ___ effort
32. Place for a necklace clasp
33. Soviet news source
36. Tachometer readings: abbr.
39. No. after a phone no.

43. Lady's title

45. Mellows, as wine

46. "You've ___ Friend" (James Taylor hit)

47. Spreadsheet lines

48. Not a good way to run

49. Hair on a horse's neck

52. Hosp. area for emergency cases

53. Kilmer of *At First Sight*

55. "Thanks, ___ no thanks"

56. Ask for alms

57. ___ Lankan

Solution on Page 274

ACROSS

1. Prickly shrub
6. "___ be my pleasure!"
9. Norm: abbr.
12. Usher's route
13. Letter after cee
14. Even if, informally
15. Gets dirty
16. Good source of dietary fiber
18. Break bread
20. Give in
21. King Arthur's home
25. Looks for
26. Not too much
27. Egyptian boy king
28. It's big in London
29. Moon vehicle, for short
31. Smoke, for short
34. He's no gentleman
37. Do a voice-over, perhaps
40. "Pet" annoyance
42. Smiled scornfully
43. Not quite
45. Texter's "Unbelievable!"
46. In-flight attendant
48. Notre Dame's Fighting ___
52. One ___ customer
53. Myrna of *The Thin Man*
54. Gently shift to a new topic
55. Busy bug
56. Reason for extra innings
57. It may be wood-burning

DOWN

1. ___-relief sculpture
2. *Blame It on* ___ (Caine comedy)
3. "It ___" (formal answer to "Who's there?")
4. Ready to go
5. Outcome
6. Altar affirmation
7. Sign of sorrow
8. Can't stand
9. San Francisco transport
10. Express gratitude to
11. Dos and ___
17. ___ cheese dressing
19. Survey
21. Part of a semi
22. Ginger ___ (soft drink)
23. Pie filling
24. They're coming of age
30. "Look ___ hands!"
32. Suffix for suburban
33. HS equivalency test
35. Openly declare
36. Treat, as seawater
38. Negligent
39. Wish undone
40. Noodles

41. Rock's ___ John

44. Enterprise counselor

47. Color, as Easter eggs

49. "Here ___ again!"

50. Popular family wheels

51. TV's ___ *Haw*

Solution on Page 274

ACROSS

1. Wee
6. Fleur-de-___
9. ___ Tome
12. Backs of necks
13. Alley in the comics
14. Film producer Roach
15. Led Zeppelin's "Whole ___ Love"
16. "Not ___ bet!"
17. Before, in poems
18. ___ Helens, Wash.
20. Talks hoarsely
22. Swear (to)
25. Tempe sch.
26. Soil-turning tool
27. Upward movement
30. Meets with
32. Irish actor Stephen
33. Musical pitch
36. Rely
38. Prime rate setter, with "the"
39. "___ in apple"
40. Debate topics
43. Admin. aides
46. Aussie buddy
47. Comedian Bernie
48. La-la intro
50. ___ salts
54. Period of history
55. Suffix with ball or bass
56. Assisted
57. Newsman Donaldson
58. TLC givers
59. Lions' dens

DOWN

1. Eddie Murphy's old show, for short
2. Chinese leader with a *Little Red Book*
3. Prone (to)
4. "___ Entertain You"
5. Exams for future attys.
6. Heist haul
7. Physics particle
8. Few and far between
9. "___ a Lady" (Tom Jones hit)
10. Over-50 grp.
11. Bullfight cries
19. Gazes steadily
21. Cousin's mother
22. Sighs of contentment
23. Stubbed extremity
24. ___ off (angry)
25. Maine's ___ National Park
28. Rep.'s counterpart
29. Bean curd
31. Goal in musical chairs
34. Maiden name intro
35. Asner and Ames
37. Congregation leader

41. Rustle, as cattle

42. Brown-toned old photo

43. Ed of *Daniel Boone*

44. "___ Smile" (Hall & Oates hit)

45. Con artist's art

46. "The way to a ___ heart…"

49. President after Jimmy

51. "Star Wars" mil. project

52. "___ the fields we go…"

53. Rx prescribers

Solution on Page 274

ACROSS

1. Leia's love
4. Scotch mixer
8. Baseball arbiter, for short
11. Once ___ blue moon
12. Gulp down
13. India's continent
14. LP successors
15. Professional org.
16. Constricting snakes
17. *Herzog* author Bellow
19. Be a snitch
21. Grown-up boys
23. War horse
26. Under debate
30. Helps with the dishes
32. Scribble (down)
33. Grand Ole Opry network
35. Opposite of pos.
36. Yellowish-brown
39. Competition
42. Truck stop stoppers
44. Suffix for shapes
45. "Get the lead out!"
47. "Take ___ a compliment"
50. "For the life ___ ..."
53. Tears
55. Dr.'s field
57. Handed-down stories
58. Lumber source
59. Toy store ___ Schwarz
60. Part of an ellipsis
61. Absorbs, with "up"
62. CAT scan alternative

DOWN

1. Hawaiian Punch alternative
2. & & &
3. Mars Pathfinder launcher
4. Musical ladders
5. Sounds of surprise
6. Do housework
7. Actress Moorehead
8. GI show sponsor
9. *Mamma ___!* (Broadway musical)
10. Faux ___ (social slip-up)
13. More competent
18. Hesitation sounds
20. Inc. alternative
22. Bolt attachment
24. German "a"
25. "Disco Duck" singer Rick
26. Double-platinum Steely Dan album
27. *Uncle ___ Cabin*
28. The Beatles' "Let ___"
29. Letter insert: abbr.
31. Friday's rank: abbr.
34. Christmas drink
37. Game show host
38. Basketball net holder

32

40. Sounds

41. Blast producer

43. Puts into piles

46. Actor Robert De ___

48. Kind of radio

49. Briefly treat with high heat

50. Part of GOP

51. Rock music's ___ Fighters

52. "I pity the fool" star

54. Verve

56. ___ look like a mind reader?

Solution on Page 274

ACROSS

1. *Silent Spring* pesticide
4. Pond organism
8. Police team acronym
12. Winning tic-tac-toe row
13. Articulates
14. *Animal House* garb
15. Buckeyes' sch.
16. ___ sapiens
17. Take ___ (snooze)
18. "Ditto"
20. Prickly plant
22. Monitor, for short
24. Big bird Down Under
25. Midpoints
29. Short-tempered
33. Eggs
34. Big fat mouth
36. Joined in matrimony
37. Material for a doctor's glove
40. Untrustworthy folks
43. Illiterates' signatures
45. HST's successor
46. Have ambitions
49. Map book
53. IRS form experts
54. Free ticket, for short
57. Mature, as wine
58. Sour
59. Relaxed running pace
60. Searched for buried treasure
61. Printers' needs
62. Maple syrup sources
63. Narc's agcy.

DOWN

1. *Indiana Jones and the Temple of ___*
2. Medicinal amount
3. Speak highly of
4. "Michael, Row the Boat ___"
5. ___ Tzu (Taoism founder)
6. Sock hop locale
7. In unison
8. Display on a pedestal
9. "I ___ Grow Up" (*Peter Pan* song)
10. "I've Got ___ in Kalamazoo"
11. Package sealer
19. Start of the fourth qtr.
21. CPR provider
23. Attempt
25. Maj.'s superior
26. Braun or Peron
27. Cole who was "King"
28. Tool with teeth
30. Stockholm's land: abbr.
31. Phone no.
32. Gridiron divs.
35. ___ XING (street sign)
38. Can be found
39. Gen-___ (boomer's kid)
41. Changes to fit

42. Tennis match segment

44. Religious factions

46. First part of a play

47. Life ___ (up to about 30 years, for a panda)

48. Place to picnic

50. Actor Alan

51. Tropical fever

52. Company whose mascot is Sonic the Hedgehog

55. "...a man ___ mouse?"

56. Unruly head of hair

Solution on Page 275

ACROSS

1. Physician's nickname
4. Part of GPA: abbr.
7. Lose, as pounds
11. Suffix like -like
12. Trawlers' gear
14. Sit
15. Negative particle
17. Pretentiously showy
18. Sums
19. Congo's cont.
21. "Well, I'll ___ monkey's uncle!"
22. Membership list
26. Earlier
29. Ryan of *Sleepless in Seattle*
30. Casper's st.
31. Smallest of a litter
32. Apt. coolers
33. Joseph's wife
34. Large deer
35. Quart parts: abbr.
36. Lessens, as pain
37. ___ Dome (Harding administration scandal)
39. "Ready, ___, fire!"
40. Tool for a lumberjack
41. Batter's position
45. Witty sorts
48. Biblical vessel
50. Don of talk radio
51. Miami-___ County, Fla.
52. ___ of war
53. Newcastle upon ___, England
54. A long way
55. Parts of lbs.

DOWN

1. Cut calories
2. Capital of Norway
3. Atkins of country music
4. Horn
5. Vice ___ (conversely)
6. Pontiac muscle car
7. Practices jabs and hooks
8. Vert. counterpart, on old TVs
9. NYC clock setting
10. Susan of *The Partridge Family*
13. Entraps
16. Explorer John or Sebastian
20. Visibility problem
23. "___ the night before Christmas…"
24. Jane of literature
25. Rogers and Orbison
26. ___-a-porter (ready-to-wear)
27. Occupy the throne
28. Durante's "___ Dinka Doo"
29. Roast hosts, briefly
32. Go to
33. The ___ and the Papas
35. Plague

36. One or the other

38. No longer fashionable

39. Carne ___ (Mexican restaurant dish)

42. Western alliance, for short

43. Texas senator Ted

44. Heart charts, for short

45. Cleverness

46. Poehler of *Parks and Recreation*

47. Rifle or revolver

49. Klutzy sort

Solution on Page 275

ACROSS

1. Sushi bar tuna
4. Burrito alternative
8. Keebler worker
11. ___ fun at (ridicule)
13. "Let's just leave ___ that"
14. Seven, on a sundial
15. *Jeopardy!* host Trebek
16. Ritzy
17. *The Addams Family* cousin
18. "Start over" button
20. Christmas tree shedding
22. Trig ratio
24. "Awesome, dude!"
25. *Ben-___* (Heston film)
28. Drug cop
30. Curtain supports
33. Scents
35. Web-footed mammals
37. "___ to help"
38. ___ Krishna
40. FF's opposite, on a VCR
41. Cable modem alternative, briefly
43. Ooze through the cracks
45. U2's "Where the ___ Have No Name"
48. Constellation components
52. Pod item
53. Throat-clearing sound
55. Each, in pricing
56. Dad's bro
57. Breathe rapidly
58. Pet adoption org.
59. Sushi eggs
60. Some explosives
61. "Needless to ___ …"

DOWN

1. On ___ with (equal to)
2. Golf target
3. Turner and Eisenhower
4. Visible part of an iceberg
5. One who makes amends
6. Part of a judge's docket
7. "On the ___ hand…"
8. Villain
9. Lo-fat
10. Is the right size
12. Divorcees
19. Turner who sang "What's Love Got to Do with It"
21. Feathered missile
23. Poet Ogden
25. Witch
26. Web address: abbr.
27. Grand Prix, e.g.
29. Rotten to the ___
31. Beats by ___ (headphones brand)
32. Away from NNE
34. Store goods: abbr.

36. Caddie's pocketful

39. Give the go-ahead

42. Sprang

44. Sch. orgs.

45. Thing on a cowboy's boot

46. "The ___'Clock News"

47. Lighter ___ air

49. PC programs

50. Almond ___ (candy brand)

51. Fix, as a cat

54. The Appalachians, e.g.: abbr.

Solution on Page 275

ACROSS

1. Sock-in-the-gut grunt
4. Very small batteries
8. Pack of cards
12. Heat measure: abbr.
13. Roger Bannister's distance
14. *Garfield* canine
15. Bro's sibling
16. Ship's front
17. Go left or right
18. Give up, as rights
20. Basic unit of heredity
22. Path of a fly ball
24. Hair-setting item
28. Interpret speech without hearing
32. ___ tectonics
33. Cubes in a freezer
34. Alehouse
36. From Jan. 1 until now, in accounting
37. Men and boys
40. Passes, as time
43. Like early audiobooks
45. OJ's alma mater
46. Supermodel Banks
48. Attack with a dagger
51. Stew holders
54. Will-___-wisp
56. Ship's front
58. Political caucus state
59. "That oughta ___!"
60. Milk source
61. Excellent, in modern slang
62. 911 responders: abbr.
63. Printer resolution meas.

DOWN

1. Baby docs, briefly
2. Of the ear
3. Firecracker part
4. Electric current unit
5. Show on TV
6. Sleep like ___
7. Underground conduit
8. "Let's hear more!"
9. College URL ending
10. Round: abbr.
11. Documentarian Burns
19. Patriotic women's org.
21. Trio before Q
23. Toothpaste topper
25. Big name in chips
26. Suffix with marion
27. Ruby and scarlet
28. It might roll up to a red carpet
29. Sammy Davis Jr.'s "Yes ___"
30. Fur trader's item
31. "Give the devil his ___"
35. ___-ray Disc
38. Bothers incessantly

39. James Bond, for one
41. Desirable qualities
42. Fractional amt.
44. Gradually wear away
47. Electron's place
49. Introductory letters?
50. Betty of comics

51. Gladys Knight backer
52. "How beautiful!"
53. Former Pan Am rival
55. Chart topper
57. It ended Nov. 11, 1918

Solution on Page 275

ACROSS

1. "___ Wiedersehen" (German "goodbye")
4. Brit. fliers
7. Spumante city
11. Univ. transcript number
12. Historical spans
14. Unhearing
15. Column's counterpart
16. Waiting room call
17. Surrealist Salvador
18. Natural
20. Eggy dish
22. Ariz. neighbor
23. Get ___ of (throw away)
24. Tick-borne disease
27. Evil spell
28. Fam. doctors
31. Knocks on the noggin
32. Year divs.
33. Ration (out)
34. Bleach container
35. Use an ax
36. From ___ (completely)
37. Cherry seed
38. Introverted
40. Put the blame on
43. Big bother
47. Motel amenity
48. One with debts

50. Too permissive
51. Philosophies
52. Barbecue entree
53. DSL provider
54. Kotter portrayer Kaplan
55. Slangy negative
56. Vietnamese noodle soup

DOWN

1. Prefix with culture
2. "___ further review…"
3. Young Bambi
4. Designer Oscar de la ___
5. Spinning dizzily
6. Send via phone line
7. Threw in
8. SeaWorld barker
9. "Tall" story
10. "___ pleases the court…"
13. Mall units
19. Unreturned tennis serves
21. Mingle
24. President after JFK
25. "___ don't say!"
26. Fuel efficiency abbr.
27. "___ about that!"
28. Received
29. West Bank grp.
30. "Oh yeah? ___ who?"
32. Space streaker

42

33. Calendar boxes

35. ___ Holiness the Pope

37. Heartbeat

38. Biblical land with a queen

39. Severe

40. Buy ___ in a poke

41. ___ Nostra

42. Hair untangler

44. "___ Slidin' Away"

45. Place for mascara

46. World's fair

49. "… ___ one for the Gipper"

Solution on Page 276

ACROSS

1. Diva's solo
5. Hourglass fill
9. Olive ___ (Popeye's sweetie)
12. Uncontrollable movements
13. ___ vera (skin soother)
14. Blvd.
15. Dian Fossey subjects
16. Cry like a baby
17. Rooster's partner
18. Longs for
20. Say "!@#$%"
21. Sun. church talk
22. Mop & ___: cleaning brand
24. Michigan or Minnesota
27. Grows molars
31. Part of a gearwheel
32. "Cut off your nose to ___ your face"
34. Homes on wheels, in brief
35. Uncomfortable spot
37. Gotten up
39. Theory suffix
40. Tin ___ Alley
41. Whispered "Hey!"
44. Hospital image
48. Cry of insight
49. City haze
51. Grammy winner Fitzgerald
52. Archaeological operation
53. Prong
54. Mon. follower
55. Wellness retreat
56. Commits perjury
57. Religious splinter group

DOWN

1. Just ___ (very little)
2. Ready to eat, as fruit
3. Chills, as champagne
4. Aid
5. Cavalry sword
6. "Sad to say…"
7. Presently
8. Wilmington's state: abbr.
9. Diamond Head's island
10. Designer St. Laurent
11. Monocle part
19. ___ Peanut Butter Cups
20. Barracks bunk
22. Understand, as a joke
23. Regard with lust
24. Learning inst.
25. Also
26. Actor's rep.
27. ___ for tat
28. Day divs.
29. Preholiday night
30. Form 1040 ID
33. Actress Dawber

36. Command to a dog

38. Maps within maps

40. Senate gofers

41. Cushions

42. Use FedEx, say

43. Multigenerational tale

44. Ice cream holder

45. Crossword hint

46. Baldwin of the silver screen

47. Political cartoonist Thomas

49. City in Mo.

50. 1,002, in old Rome

Solution on Page 276

ACROSS

1. Streisand nickname
5. Playwright George Bernard
9. Small bit
12. At the drop of ___ (quickly)
13. Old king of rhyme
14. Prefix with puncture
15. "Alas!"
16. "___ boy!" ("Way to go!")
17. Kind
18. Rental dwellings: abbr.
20. What it's worth
22. Digging tool
25. 100 yrs.
26. Contented sigh
27. Popeye's tooter
30. Pained cry
34. Heating fuel
35. Borders
37. Scooby-___ (cartoon dog)
38. Greek love god
40. Cellar dweller's position
41. Alternative to .com or .net
42. 180 from NNW
44. Tall tales
46. Somewhat, informally
49. Rowing team
51. Impress greatly
52. Princess who battles the Death Star
54. Prefix meaning "height"
58. Part of a min.
59. Telegraphed
60. Perlman of *Cheers*
61. DDE's predecessor
62. "Pale" drinks
63. Rolltop, for one

DOWN

1. Cry to Bo-Peep
2. "That feels good!"
3. "Kapow!"
4. Stand in good ___
5. "Get lost, kitty!"
6. Red ___ (cinnamon candies)
7. Ctrl-___-Del
8. Zig and zag
9. Lobster serving
10. Rights grp.
11. Home of the Blue Devils
19. Cartoon skunk Le Pew
21. "A rose by ___ other name…"
22. Wise one
23. Carson's predecessor
24. Charlie Chan's comment
25. Average marks
28. Sit in neutral
29. Tiger Woods's org.
31. It stinks
32. Threadbare
33. Captains' records

46

36. Eyelid annoyance

39. Retired fast plane: abbr.

43. Chip dip

45. Prize

46. Miss America band

47. Is indebted to

48. Four-sided fig.

49. French film

50. Charlie Brown's "Darn!"

53. Fish that might shock you

55. Fighter with Fidel

56. Hi-___ monitor

57. Tree with acorns

Solution on Page 276

ACROSS

1. 401(k) alternatives
5. Tree with cones
8. Gillette razor brand
12. Speeder's penalty
13. Military mail drop: abbr.
14. Goatee site
15. Went like the dickens
16. Lassie's mate
17. Unwakable state
18. "Should ___ acquaintance…"
20. Grinch creator
21. Numerical data
24. Wet dirt
25. Broadcast
26. Church bell spot
30. Investigator: abbr.
31. Loud commotion
32. Like most sushi
33. Made an attempt
36. Pilotless plane
38. Coffee order: abbr.
39. Office furniture
40. Underlying principle
43. Plate
45. Metallic rocks
46. Foil metal
47. "Don't have ___, man!"
51. "The stockings ___ hung…"
52. Florist's vehicle
53. iPhone assistant
54. Places for experiments
55. Complete jerk
56. *Bonanza* son

DOWN

1. Contingencies
2. Tear (up)
3. "Gimme ___!" (end of a Yale cheer)
4. Tranquilize
5. Autumn
6. Apple tablet computer
7. Serling or Stewart
8. Give in
9. "___ shalt not steal"
10. What swish shots miss
11. Santa ___ (hot California winds)
19. Amer. currency unit
20. Be litigious
21. "The Sweetest Taboo" singer
22. What extra innings break
23. The "A" in BA
24. Matterhorn, e.g.: abbr.
26. Punk rocker Vicious
27. Paid players
28. Long and lean
29. Providers of sheep's milk
31. Univ. offering
34. Gets up
35. Word of accord

48

36. Shingle letters
37. Go over again
40. Knock down some pins
41. Carpet measurement
42. Kosovo War participant
43. "Buenos ___"
44. Rustic retreats

46. New Deal dam-building org.
48. AFL's partner
49. Hospital areas: abbr.
50. The Badger St.

Solution on Page 276

ACROSS

1. ___ *Pinafore*
4. Creme ___ creme
8. Casino token
12. Very long time
13. Gave a thumbs-up
14. Incantation start
15. Batman and Robin are a "dynamic" one
16. Mellowed
17. Dawdling
18. Antelope seen on safaris
19. Remove from a mother's milk
21. Jazzy singer ___ James
23. Armed conflicts
24. Plastic pipe material
27. Fay of the original *King Kong*
29. Canary call
31. Alpine dwelling
34. "___, My God, to Thee"
35. Rapper's entourage
36. Put on ___ (be snobbish)
37. "___ du lieber!"
38. Rhett Butler's last word
40. ___ de foie gras
44. "Woe ___!"
45. Superman archvillain Luthor
46. Cries of contempt
49. Clever tactic
52. Clerk on *The Simpsons*
53. Teheran's nation
54. ___ of the party
55. Fam. member
56. "Think nothing ___!"
57. "I could ___ horse!"
58. "Have we ___?"

DOWN

1. Botanical fence
2. ___ Rushmore
3. Animal nose
4. Too late for the ER
5. Heart chart, for short
6. Wiggle room
7. Viper
8. ___ Crunch (Quaker cereal)
9. *The Sopranos* network
10. Nettle
11. Take care of a bill
20. Fall flower
22. Hole-punching tools
23. Angkor ___ (Cambodian temple)
24. Part of RPM
25. "Rubber Ball" singer Bobby
26. Middle: abbr.
28. Oboes and bassoons
30. Stinging insect
31. Number cruncher, for short
32. Ad ___ committee
33. Volcanic emission

34. Palindromic diarist

36. Aviator Earhart

39. More than enough

41. Car security device

42. Sioux shelter

43. Rejoice

44. "Winning ___ everything"

46. Brief life story?

47. Comics bark

48. Japanese "yes"

50. Frequently, in poetry

51. Opposite of nay

Solution on Page 277

ACROSS

1. Grad student's mentor
5. Corp. boss
8. Uneven hairdo
12. Cry from Santa
13. Noun modifier: abbr.
14. When tripled, a WWII movie
15. Some PCs
16. Enlisted soldiers, briefly
17. Share a border with
18. Popeye's ___' Pea
20. $100 bill, slangily
21. *Andrea* ___ (ill-fated ship)
24. Prof.'s degree
25. Entirely
26. Van Gogh subjects
29. Gym iteration
30. Cloud locale
31. Oft-tattooed word
33. Suppress
36. Signs of things to come
38. Bashful
39. "What's the ___ that can happen?"
40. Texas A&M student
43. ___ Alto, Calif.
45. Part in a movie
46. Jan. follower
47. In need of a map
51. Greek god of war
52. File folder projection
53. Bush's "___ of evil"
54. Not straight
55. Moistureless
56. Exchange for fast cash

DOWN

1. ___ Beta Kappa
2. Burglarize
3. Electrical unit
4. Paleontologist's find
5. Actor Nicolas of *The Rock*
6. *The Sopranos* Emmy winner Falco
7. Citrus drinks, for short
8. Prepares for the anthem
9. Boxcar rider
10. Stuck in ___
11. Entryway
19. ___mart (retail chain)
20. Greek letter X
21. N, E, W, or S
22. Smallest bills
23. Riveted with attention
24. Be nosy
26. Mike & ___ (candy brand)
27. Like a 911 call: abbr.
28. *My Three* ___
30. Crafty
32. Denver clock setting: abbr.
34. Most frigid
35. Hostile force

Puzzle 22

36. Night bird

37. Simoleons

40. Mideast native

41. Al or Tipper

42. "Rhinestone Cowboy" singer Campbell

43. Fall fruit

44. "Dear" advice giver

46. 1-800-FLOWERS rival

48. Kitchen gadget brand

49. [not my mistake]

50. Sound of disapproval

Solution on Page 277

ACROSS

1. Polite
6. Tel Aviv's land: abbr.
9. Spanish day
12. In the cooler
13. Barnyard sound
14. Off-road transport, for short
15. Follows directions
16. Young seal
17. ___ tai
18. Blueprint detail
20. Animation art pieces
21. Ghostly greeting
24. Schiller's "___ Joy"
26. Letters between K and O
27. Runner Sebastian
28. Playwright Chekhov
32. Amorously inflame
34. Safeguard
35. Informal eatery
36. Droop in the middle
37. Feline zodiac sign
38. Peru's peaks
40. Chaney of film
41. Mgr.'s helper
44. Marsh grass
46. Cheerleader's syllable
47. Sandwich meat
48. Photo book
53. Waitress at Mel's Diner
54. Binary code digit
55. Miss America's crown
56. Engine additive letters
57. Deity
58. Examination of accounts

DOWN

1. Make dove sounds
2. Bach's Mass ___ Minor
3. Try (for)
4. Slippery, as a road
5. More or ___ (to some extent)
6. Get in the way of
7. Hollandaise, e.g.
8. Jay-Z's genre
9. *The Hunchback of Notre* ___
10. Slanted in print: abbr.
11. "We try harder" company
19. Destitute
20. Hoodwinks
21. Ran in the wash
22. Old Dodge
23. "Chestnuts roasting ___ open fire"
25. Tart taste
27. It's grown in ears
29. Rock's Jethro ___
30. Popular sandwich cookie
31. Advertising sign gas
33. Butcher's offering
34. Lighten up

36. Appeared to be
39. Liquid-Plumr rival
41. Barks
42. Popcorn seasoning
43. Boutique
45. Computer input or output
47. Harley-Davidson, slangily

49. Lucy of *Kill Bill*
50. Awful
51. Geller who claims paranormal ability
52. Yoga class surface

Solution on Page 277

ACROSS

1. Degrees held by many CEOs
5. Rock concert blaster
8. Cleansing agent
12. "This round's ___!"
13. British john
14. Homecoming attendee, for short
15. Extremely narrow, as a shoe
16. Complimentary ticket
18. Windshield glare reducer
19. NBA tiebreakers
20. Hits the slopes
23. Smooths wood
28. Hole-making tool
31. Vigoda and Lincoln
33. Bluish green
34. *Jane Eyre* author
36. Montana's capital
38. Pleads
39. New Mexico town on the Santa Fe Trail
41. Maze-running rodent
42. Lend ___ (listen)
44. House members, for short
46. Deep anger
48. *Fargo* director
52. Type of pregame party
57. Thomas ___ Edison
58. Top-rated
59. ___ sequitur
60. "I've ___ had!"
61. Barely makes, with "out"
62. Viscous substance
63. Not great, but not awful either

DOWN

1. Ring of water
2. ___ B'rith
3. To ___ (unanimously)
4. Auditorium row units
5. Furry sitcom alien
6. Moody
7. Verse writer
8. Maple tree fluid
9. Pay or Cray ending
10. Neighbor of Ger.
11. Tony Blair and others, briefly
17. Curved letter
21. Krazy ___ of the comics
22. Sarcastic agreement
24. US/UK divider
25. "... ___ the twain shall meet"
26. *The X-Files* agent Scully
27. Blinds crosspiece
28. "Mamma Mia" singing group
29. Chirpy bird
30. Theater section
32. Nike product
35. CIA relative
37. Paranormal ability, for short

Puzzle 24

40. "Am not!" rejoinder
43. Fix illegally
45. Picket line crossers
47. Tolled, as a bell
49. Butter-like spread
50. Pre-holiday nights
51. iPod type

52. ___ kwon do (martial art)
53. Fine and dandy
54. Suffix with serpent
55. ___ Paul guitars
56. British rocker Brian

Solution on Page 277

ACROSS

1. Cops enforce them
5. ___ a plea
8. Tell all
12. Nastase of tennis
13. Hoops org.
14. Civil rights pioneer Parks
15. Tiny biter
16. Zilch
17. Scheduled mtg.
18. Online crafts marketplace
19. Slithery fish
21. ___ Lingus (Irish airline)
24. Perfume compound
28. San Francisco's ___ Hill
31. Searches (through)
34. "… ___ quit!"
35. "Honor ___ father and…"
36. Apple centers
37. Wire measurement
38. Recently stolen
39. Do penance (for)
40. Pollen collector
41. Mutton source
43. Welby and Kildare: abbr.
45. Garden plots
48. Lassies' partners
52. Heights: abbr.
55. How some stocks are sold: abbr.
57. Fit to ___
58. Put together
59. Jean-___ Picard
60. Leaning Tower's city
61. ___ the ground floor
62. Ozs. and ozs.
63. Washer cycle

DOWN

1. Key ___ pie
2. Came to rest on a wire, e.g.
3. Ingenuity
4. "Later!"
5. Atlanta's ___ Center
6. New York theater award
7. Hardly tanned
8. Word with tacks or knuckles
9. Chop off
10. Venomous viper
11. Belfry flier
20. Like one of two evils
22. Break out
23. Unruly outbreak
25. ___ of the Unknown Soldier
26. One of the Great Lakes
27. Make mad
28. Extreme degrees
29. Words of surprise
30. Eight bits
32. To and ___ (back and forth)
33. Care for

58

42. *Barnaby Jones* star Buddy

44. High-fives

46. Raggedy Ann, e.g.

47. Half a ticket

49. "Let me give you ___"

50. Arnaz of *I Love Lucy*

51. Penn or Connery

52. "___ my brother's keeper?"

53. PC linkup

54. Boxing ref's call

56. Syringe amts.

Solution on Page 278

ACROSS

1. Fills with wonder
5. Pennies: abbr.
8. CIO partner
11. Breathing sound
12. Motor City org.
13. "See you later!"
14. Tennis score after deuce
15. Pre-P three
16. Appends
17. Poke fun at
19. School break
21. Terminate
23. Play-___ (kiddie clay)
24. Source of a licorice-like flavoring
28. Tennis champ Monica
32. Martial arts expert Bruce
33. "That's ___ funny!"
35. Prefix with thermal or metric
36. Analyze, as a sentence
39. Calms
42. ___ *Just Not That Into You* (2004 bestseller)
44. Gross minus expenses
45. Avenue
48. Wood strips
52. Put bullets in
53. Suffix with dull or drunk
56. Peek add-on
57. Flubs
58. Breathtaking snake
59. Aberdeen native
60. Never say this
61. Holy Trinity member
62. Head-shakers' syllables

DOWN

1. "I smell ___!"
2. Walk through water
3. *The Last Tycoon* director Kazan
4. Hearing and sight
5. Magna ___ laude
6. Camel's color
7. Dueling weapon
8. Senate staffer
9. Short-lived fashions
10. Profit's opposite
13. Secret stash
18. 180 from WSW
20. Canon camera named for a goddess
22. Cub Scout unit
24. Yodeler's perch
25. Teachers' org.
26. Suffix with cash
27. Hair arrangements
29. Ignited, as a match
30. 180 from WNW
31. Maritime distress signal
34. Toe count

37. Outbuildings

38. Wide shoe width

40. *The ___ Moines Register*

41. "It's about time!"

43. ___ in the back (betrays)

45. Toboggan, e.g.

46. Spelling of *Beverly Hills, 90210*

47. Pinkish, as a steak

49. What tots are taught

50. Borrowed without permission

51. Drunkards

54. Australian hopper, for short

55. Dapper ___

Solution on Page 278

ACROSS

1. 24-hr. cash source
4. Comedian DeLuise
7. Croon
11. ___ sauce
12. Clapton of rock
14. Neighbor of Thailand
15. Family members
16. Hawaiian nut
18. ___ Island Ferry
20. "Walk, don't ___!"
21. Move one's tail
22. Lure into crime
26. Like sea water
29. Flavorful seed
30. Card game akin to crazy eights
31. Chili ___ carne
32. "I'll be right there!"
36. Passwords provide it
39. "Hot" Mexican food
40. "Mazel ___!"
41. Spanish hero El ___
42. Hound
46. One who can see what you're saying
50. Lao ___ (Chinese philosopher)
51. Painful boo-boo
52. Flagmaker Betsy
53. Spherical body
54. Agent 007
55. Former rival of AT&T
56. "I ___ afraid of that!"

DOWN

1. Puts a question to
2. "There's nothing ___!" ("Easy!")
3. Talking bird
4. Abase
5. Juice source
6. What a DJ speaks into
7. Leans
8. "___ the Walrus"
9. "___ won't be afraid" ("Stand by Me" lyric)
10. Fed. property overseer
13. Shows concern
17. Sand hill
19. Light opening?
23. 10K or marathon
24. Andy's pal on old radio
25. Writing tools
26. Business attire
27. *The King and I* tutor
28. Gardener's soil
33. Like cows, to Hindus
34. 1986 Nobel Peace Prize winner Wiesel
35. Closet wood
36. Under the most favorable circumstances

37. Not fine-grained

38. Walgreens rival

43. Store, as a ship's cargo

44. Poet Pound

45. Bath fixtures

46. High arcing shot

47. ___ Jima

48. Wrestler's objective

49. Hound

Solution on Page 278

ACROSS

1. Boozer
4. Nighttime twinkler
8. Fill-in for a striking worker
12. Jackie O's husband
13. Spare in a trunk
14. "Mary ___ Little Lamb"
15. Decreased
17. "This thing weighs ___!"
18. Final or midterm
19. "We hold ___ truths…"
20. Place to sit
23. Managed care gps.
25. Come in behind the others
26. Fannie ___ (securities)
27. ___-K (toddlers' school)
30. Juneau's state
32. Lay into
34. Fellow
35. Meg of *In the Cut*
37. Choose
38. Letterman's "Top Ten," e.g.
39. Ocean motions
40. Infants
43. Like a wafer
45. "It's ___ misunderstanding"
46. Circle bisector
50. Wall St. debuts
51. "Do it, or ___!"
52. Primate
53. Reusable bag
54. Wrestling surfaces
55. Soup container

DOWN

1. *My Gal* ___
2. Mining find
3. Opposite of 'tain't
4. Beef animal
5. Cookie containers
6. Franklin known as the Queen of Soul
7. Ketchup-colored
8. Former Iranian rulers
9. Actress Blanchett
10. Bustles
11. Curse
16. Pigpens
19. Mix, as a salad
20. Chowder ingredient
21. Spanish greeting
22. As strong ___ ox
24. Downright nasty
26. Baseball great Willie
27. Picked up the tab
28. Sushi ingredient
29. Moose cousins
31. ___ Kringle
33. Backbone
36. Famous Hun

38. Renter's paper

39. Multiplied by

40. Angler's need

41. Brand for Bowser

42. Ink stain

44. "…why ___ thou forsaken me?"

46. Rep.'s foe

47. Tic ___ (mint)

48. Govt. pollution watchdog

49. Stimpy's cartoon buddy

Solution on Page 278

ACROSS

1. Computer's core, briefly
4. Like an unmatched sock
7. Give this for that
11. Go like a bunny
12. Disfigure
14. Lima's country
15. Licorice-flavored liqueur
17. Fox Sports alternative
18. Go back on one's word
19. *20/20* network
21. Parental palindrome
22. Actress Sarandon
25. Actress ___ Pinkett Smith
28. Go by plane
29. Level out the lawn
31. Victor's cry
32. ___ an egg (flop)
33. Safari sound
34. Atlas page
35. Mary ___ cosmetics
36. Military force
37. Affirmative votes
39. Dutch airline
41. Strong alkali
42. Katmandu resident
46. Be furious
49. Brightness regulator
51. Company with a crocodile logo
52. Glimpsed
53. Idiot boxes
54. Jar tops
55. Miami's state: abbr.
56. "___, team!"

DOWN

1. Blacken, as steak
2. Corn bread
3. Go ___ smoke
4. ___-3 fatty acids
5. Went out with
6. Bit of Morse code
7. Glasses, informally
8. *Fantastic Mr. Fox* director Anderson
9. Dada artist Jean
10. Bit of wordplay
13. Pathetically small
16. Alternative to a station wagon or convertible
20. Pay for
23. "Love," in Latin
24. Author Chomsky
25. Muppeteer Henson
26. "___ in a Manger"
27. Narc's seizure
28. Wray of *King Kong*
30. Lopsided, as a grin
32. Surgical beams
33. Stadium walkways

35. F major or E minor

38. Toboggans

39. Prepare to be knighted

40. Helmsley of hotels

43. Lawyer: abbr.

44. Liquid rock

45. Teeny, informally

46. Chick-___-A (fast-food chain)

47. Israeli arm

48. Chic, to Austin Powers

50. *Playboy* founder, familiarly

Solution on Page 279

ACROSS

1. Piece of glass
5. Hosp. triage areas
8. Billy the ___
11. Altar vows
12. Morse code sound
13. ___-Soviet relations
14. Pub serving
15. ___ Khan (Islamic title)
16. "Don't look ___ like that!"
17. Daubs
19. Gets the soap off
21. Coal measure
22. Beetle Bailey's rank: abbr.
23. Strikes out
27. Oregon's capital
31. Nasdaq debut: abbr.
32. Symbol for Aries
34. Square root of IX
35. Falafel holders
38. Drives recklessly
41. Bacardi, e.g.
43. NFL Hall of Famer Dawson
44. Bathhouse
47. Is of use to
51. Just ___ (small amount, as of hair gel)
52. "...or ___ thought"
54. Cyberspace conversation
55. Stage show backgrounds
56. Cries of pain
57. Heavy volume
58. Sneaky laugh sound
59. U-turn from SSW
60. Erupt

DOWN

1. Domino spots
2. Take ___ view of (frown on)
3. Opposite of all
4. Subject of a will
5. Lou Grant portrayer
6. Dishcloth
7. Quick-witted
8. Hobby shop purchases
9. "I didn't know I had it ___!"
10. Bucks' mates
13. Christmas visitor
18. Go beyond ripe
20. ER hookups
23. Quick swim
24. Prefix with dermis
25. Developer's site
26. Baglike structure
28. Pinocchio's undoing
29. "Ich bin ___ Berliner": JFK
30. Wrong: prefix
33. Listlessness
36. Saudis, e.g.
37. Solar system center

68

39. Gun a motor

40. Passes, as a law

42. Bricklayer

44. Money on hand

45. "Zip-___-Doo-Dah"

46. Relaxing soak

48. Denny's alternative

49. Totally uncool

50. Cook, as tomatoes

53. Rent-to-___

Solution on Page 279

ACROSS

1. In a merry mood
4. Undecorated
8. "If I Only ___ a Brain"
11. Numbered musical work
13. Of the mouth
14. Earth-friendly prefix
15. Cotton unit
16. Crossword pattern
17. Nostalgic vocal group ___ Na Na
18. Cardiologist's insert
20. Some are bitter or sworn
22. Brings to court
24. Like many seniors: abbr.
25. Airwaves regulatory gp.
28. Cole and Turner
30. Place for a crow's nest
33. Mistake remover
35. Handsome lad of myth
37. Sported
38. Glamorous actress Turner
40. Uno + due
41. Calif. neighbor
43. Morning moistures
45. "___ the Beautiful"
48. ___ decongestant
52. Graffiti signature
53. McDonald's arches, e.g.
55. ___ record
56. "Lord, is ___?" (Last Supper question)
57. Pork cut
58. Piggy-bank aperture
59. ___ *Sun Also Rises*
60. Mil. mail centers
61. Agent's 15%, e.g.

DOWN

1. Lots
2. Get ___ on the back
3. Christmas season
4. Peat source
5. Slap the cuffs on
6. Drops from the sky
7. Church officer
8. Wavering
9. Muscle pain
10. "When in Rome, ___ the Romans…"
12. DC 100: abbr.
19. Jukebox choice
21. Workplace communication
23. ___ Grey tea
25. ___ and far between
26. ___-Magnon
27. "The Steel King" Andrew
29. Sound of mind
31. Title for a knight
32. Taoism founder Lao ___

70

Puzzle 31

34. Psychic

36. First light

39. Slowly, in music

42. Country retreat

44. Bratty talk

45. Hard ___ (toiling away)

46. SAT section

47. Hen pen

49. Egotist's love

50. Stick ___ in the water

51. Not in time

54. Carry-___ (small pieces of luggage)

Solution on Page 279

ACROSS

1. Treasury secretary Geithner
4. E.g., e.g.
8. Poke
12. VW predecessors?
13. Disney's ___ & *Stitch*
14. Closely related (to)
15. HP products
16. "...more than one way to skin ___"
17. 7-Up alternative
18. Luster
20. In this place
22. Flash drive port
24. Curved
28. Wild hog
31. ___-poly
34. Lacto-___ vegetarian
35. Mos. and mos.
36. Stares open-mouthed
37. Rug cleaner, for short
38. *Charlotte's Web* author's monogram
39. Concerning
40. Sloppy condition
41. Run-down
43. Complain, complain, complain
45. Not bogus
48. Huge hit
52. Org. for women on the links
55. Runs for exercise
57. When repeated, a ballroom dance
58. Drench
59. Have ___ with
60. Announcer Pardo
61. Suggest strongly
62. Rules, for short
63. Fish and chips fish

DOWN

1. Dosage amts.
2. Result of a mosquito bite
3. Inspiration source
4. Greenspan and Arkin
5. Ballpoint brand
6. Washed-out feeling
7. Repetitive learning method
8. Indiana basketballer
9. *Top Hat* studio
10. Engine lubricant
11. Paternity proof, briefly
19. Afr. neighbor
21. Sunbathers catch them
23. Bosom companions
25. Shoreline indentation
26. Braun and Gabor
27. Physicians, briefly
28. Farewells
29. Kill ___ killed (law of the jungle)
30. "... ___ forgive our debtors"
32. ___ out (decline)
33. Spinks or Trotsky

36. "Let's Get It On" singer

40. Vegas's ___ Grand

42. Male duck

44. Orgs.

46. Not completely shut

47. Like Texas's star

49. "Back in Black" band

50. "Scram, fly!"

51. You may lend it to someone

52. Baton Rouge sch.

53. ___ favor

54. "___ me with a spoon!"

56. Band booking

Solution on Page 279

ACROSS

1. Knights' titles
5. Screen siren Gardner
8. Sailor's mop
12. Winslet of *Titanic*
13. Prosecutors, briefly
14. Outfielder's cry
15. "Haven't ___ you somewhere before?"
16. And others, for short
17. "Thanks ___!"
18. One of the five senses
20. Flew high
22. Long.'s opposite
24. Rat-a-___
25. Heaven's gatekeeper
29. Ed of *Lou Grant*
33. How-___ (instructional books)
34. 24 hours
36. Fleming who created James Bond
37. Involuntary twitch
40. Crooner Frank
43. Driveway surface
45. Word paired with "neither"
46. Sees eye to eye
49. Rope fiber
53. Ready and willing companion
54. Firms: abbr.
56. Like Lindbergh's flight
57. Negative votes
58. Sick ___ dog
59. Wart causer, in legend
60. Thumbs-up votes
61. Place for notes
62. Girl of Green Gables

DOWN

1. Short sketch
2. "___ Rock" (Simon & Garfunkel hit)
3. 66 and others: abbr.
4. Come to terms
5. Fruity cooler
6. Vintners' vessels
7. High-class tie
8. Horse sense
9. ___ E. Coyote
10. "With a wink and ___"
11. Play the ponies
19. End a hunger strike
21. Roadside assistance org.
23. Turner who founded CNN
25. Urban roads: abbr.
26. Apex
27. Free TV ad, for short
28. ___ Tafari
30. Tiny criticism
31. Hearing organ
32. Gene material, in brief
35. ___ and yang
38. Emphasize

39. Daisy or Fannie

41. Turndowns

42. Competitor of Capitol and Epic

44. Summary

46. "It's ___!" (birth announcement)

47. "As they shouted out with ___ ..."

48. Slugger Sammy

50. In short order

51. Shepard who walked on the moon

52. Rich vein

53. Santa ___, Calif.

55. In a blue mood

Solution on Page 280

ACROSS

1. Lend a hand
5. Roman 300
8. Refine, as flour
12. Gas or elec.
13. "Well, that's obvious!"
14. Time ___ half
15. Rikki-Tikki-___ (Kipling mongoose)
16. EMS procedure
17. Cincinnati sitcom station
18. Prepare, as tea
20. Brainpower stats
22. ___ *from the Past*
25. Stovetop item
28. Lump in the throat
31. Humiliation
33. "Gee willikers!"
34. Four-poster, e.g.
36. Operating system developed at Bell Labs
37. Dental care brand
39. Least cooked
41. "Oy ___!"
42. Potato pancake
44. Station that uses veejays
45. Deep gorge
50. Microwave, slangily
53. Authorizes
56. "Am ___ early?"
57. Obviously eager
58. Seek the affections of
59. Cleopatra's river
60. Stop!
61. Half a dozen
62. Turner and Danson

DOWN

1. *Gilligan's Island* dwellings
2. Coup d'___
3. Not taped
4. Ballerina's knee bend
5. Atlanta-based public health agcy.
6. Putter's target
7. Evert of tennis
8. Wood-cutting tools
9. Pen filler
10. New Deal pres.
11. Keg attachment
19. Big Bird's network
21. Oil amts.
23. Women's ___
24. Danger signal
25. Partner of pots
26. Exclude
27. Singing cowboy Ritter
28. Ripped apart
29. Start of "The Star-Spangled Banner"
30. Rink org.
32. Color gradation
33. White House URL suffix
35. N. ___ (Fargo's state, for short)

38. Three-letter sandwich

40. ___ room (place to play games)

43. Declares openly

44. ___ Millions (multistate lottery)

46. Help for the stumped

47. Play to ___ (draw)

48. Realtor's favorite sign

49. *The Simpsons* tavern

50. Slangy refusal

51. "That's disgusting!"

52. "Rock and Roll, Hoochie ___" (1974 hit)

54. Colorful pond fish

55. Boston Red ___

Solution on Page 280

ACROSS

1. "Pipe down!"
4. High-end German cars
8. Close loudly
12. Hyundai rival
13. Plumbing problem
14. El ___ (weather phenomenon)
15. Relatives of egos
16. Cockeyed
17. ___'acte (intermission)
18. Prickly seed cover
20. Stockholm natives
22. Overlook's offering
26. Give and take?
27. Desserts with crusts
28. Brain scans, briefly
30. Menacing sight in *Jaws*
31. ___ City Rollers
32. D–H connection
35. Hayloft's location
36. Black-tie party
37. Expire, as a subscription
41. Brand-new business
43. Time-honored
45. "Casual" dress day: abbr.
46. ___ Mountains (Eurasian range)
47. "This is the thanks ___?"
50. *Friends* network
53. Tenth: prefix
54. Bad habit
55. Capote, familiarly
56. Plant-to-be
57. MIT grad
58. Old California fort

DOWN

1. Move on snow
2. Kept under wraps
3. One whose star is dimmed
4. Trumpet sound
5. Kitten call
6. "All's fair" in it
7. "The ___ the limit!"
8. Evil smile
9. Singer Ronstadt
10. Chipped in chips
11. Samuel with a code
19. Young ___ (tykes)
21. Ozs. and lbs.
22. Letters on a Coppertone bottle
23. 102, in old Rome
24. Country crooner McEntire
25. Months and months
29. *Peer* ___ (Ibsen play)
32. Erode
33. Annual vaccine target
34. Generation ___
35. Actress Barbara ___ Geddes
36. Dog's warning
37. Praises highly

78

38. Share the same opinion

39. War's opposite

40. ___ as a rock

42. "And Jill came tumbling ___"

44. Emulate Greg Louganis

48. Tonic go-with

49. Heart chart: abbr.

51. "It's freezing!"

52. What a cow chews

Solution on Page 280

ACROSS

1. Early hrs.
4. Hit the runway
8. Wander about
12. It may be hard on a construction worker
13. Chew persistently
14. Opposite of ecto-
15. High rank
17. Title fish in a Pixar film
18. Suffix with million or billion
19. Votes into office
21. Partner of cease
23. "Scram!"
26. Part of NFL: abbr.
28. Underground Railroad "passenger"
29. Takes too much of, in a way
32. Shuts tightly
34. "Losing My Religion" band
35. Property claims
37. Prohibits
39. Roasts' hosts
41. Samples
45. Secondhand shop deal
47. Seeing red
48. Dragged to court
50. Lamp fuel
52. Initial poker stake
53. Indiana senator Bayh
54. ___ Tin Tin
55. Even, scorewise
56. Farm storage building
57. ___ Speedwagon (1970s–1980s band)

DOWN

1. Leading in the game
2. Mrs. Eisenhower
3. Mixes
4. Big: abbr.
5. Actress Bening
6. Table salt, to a chemist
7. Uncool one
8. Avis offering
9. Poor movie rating
10. USN bigwig
11. Stockyard call
16. Dresden denial
20. Big name in small planes
22. Talks back to
24. "So ___ heard"
25. President pro ___
27. Experimentation station
29. Cry for a matador
30. Slow-witted
31. Give off, like pheromones
33. Gridiron pitchout
36. Couldn't do without
38. Sound of a leak
40. Rice wines

42. "___ is human…"

43. Country singer Tennessee ___ Ford

44. "___ evil, hear…"

46. ___ Strauss & Co.

48. Pre-coll. exam

49. Prefix with cycle

51. Beatle bride Yoko

Solution on Page 280

ACROSS

1. 11th graders: abbr.
4. Weep loudly
7. Shoulder bag feature
12. Center of a hurricane
13. Basketball's ___ Ming
14. Caribbean resort island
15. They're in your apartment building
17. Piano technician
18. Pampering, for short
19. Nap in Oaxaca
20. Not a reproduction: abbr.
22. Salacious glance
24. Pre-stereo
25. And so forth
30. Part of NA
31. Feminine pronoun
32. Lemon and lime drinks
33. Set free
35. Person from Bangkok
36. *Pretty Woman* star Richard
37. Spigots
38. ___ the Ides of March
42. Tit ___ tat
43. Stood up
44. Approve
48. Fire sign
49. "There but for the grace of God ___"
50. On the sick list
51. Dieter's lunch
52. Big inits. in trucks
53. June grads: abbr.

DOWN

1. Boeing 747, e.g.
2. Seeded bread
3. Watchtower guard
4. In ___ (coordinated)
5. Cheerios ingredient
6. Derek and Diddley
7. Lampoon
8. ___ *Grit* (John Wayne film)
9. Seeks office
10. Help in a holdup
11. Prefix with medic
16. 2000 candidate
19. Withdraw (from)
20. Bridge master Sharif
21. *La Dolce Vita* setting
22. Apartment dweller
23. Bygone anesthetic
26. Skin art
27. John Glenn portrayer in *The Right Stuff*
28. Gather what's been sown
29. Caveat emptor phrase
34. Shook hands (on)
38. Striped fish
39. Humor columnist Bombeck

82

40. Winter coat material

41. "May I ___ silly question?"

42. Savings acct. protector

44. Cadbury confection

45. ___ de plume (pen name)

46. Camera type, briefly

47. Pro golfer Ernie

Solution on Page 281

ACROSS

1. Societies: abbr.
5. ___-European (language group)
9. Apparel for a young diner
12. It may be rolled out in the rain
13. Short-order pro
14. ___ Dhabi
15. Cake decorator
16. Yelled
18. Precursor of reggae
19. Getz or Kenton
20. Knight, dame, etc.
24. Postal delivery
28. Blue feeling
30. Moisten the turkey
31. Speechified
32. Tyrant
33. Sheets, pillowcases, etc.
34. ___ Palace
35. Adam and Eve's garden
36. Make a difference
37. ___ to none (long odds)
39. Broadway play segment
42. Soothed
46. Frankenstein's assistant
47. Brother of Curly and Shemp
48. Infamous Roman emperor
49. Fool
50. CBS forensic series
51. Snatch
52. "Do as ___, not…"

DOWN

1. Redding who sang "The Dock of the Bay"
2. ___ of lamb
3. Large, powerful dog
4. Easter season: abbr.
5. German "I"
6. Hangmen's ropes
7. Blockheads
8. Neighbor of Tex.
9. ___ and grill
10. "When Will ___ Loved"
11. Blossom-to-be
17. As a group
21. Passionate
22. Many a new driver
23. '60s hallucinogenic
25. Vegetable that comes in spears
26. "Love ___ leave it"
27. Reply to "Shall we?"
28. Lone
29. Desert-dry
30. Borscht vegetable
32. Not dis
34. Picture taker
36. Tightwad
38. Singer k.d.
40. Nightclub in a Manilow song

41. Three, in cards

42. Cable film channel

43. Opposite of neg.

44. Shar-___ (wrinkly dog)

45. Driver's license stat.

46. Uganda's Amin

Solution on Page 281

ACROSS

1. 201, to Caesar
4. "Be that ___ may…"
8. "Is there ___ against that?"
12. Time Warner spin-off of '09
13. Song word repeated after "Que"
14. Kind of dancer
15. Fa follower
16. Beauty parlor
18. No longer fresh
20. HS seniors' exams
21. NFL scores
22. Pundits' pieces
26. Brother of Cain and Seth
28. Genghis ___
31. Going by way of
32. Mauna ___
33. Tractor maker John
34. Our lang.
35. ___ Cruces, New Mexico
36. Folklore beast
37. Veep's superior
38. Violinist Isaac
40. Moms
41. Detroit product
44. Preferred invitees
47. Tom Sawyer's creator
51. Recent: prefix
52. Bait and switch, e.g.
53. "___ from Muskogee"
54. Dee's predecessor
55. Some noncoms: abbr.
56. Tax form IDs
57. Els's followers

DOWN

1. Mama of the Mamas and the Papas
2. Codger
3. Nervously uncomfortable
4. Fireplace remnants
5. Large body of water
6. Eye-color area
7. *Gone with the Wind* estate
8. Audibly shocked
9. Online shorthand in reply to a joke
10. "A long time ___ in a galaxy far, far away…"
11. Was victorious
17. Rosetta ___
19. "Bad" cholesterol letters
23. From then on
24. Eat fancily
25. Droops
26. Cure-___ (panaceas)
27. Dinghy or dory
28. Beer barrel
29. That woman
30. "How ___ you?"
33. Pastry with a hole

37. Bert, to Ernie

39. Gathers leaves

40. Lions' locks

42. Pairs

43. Acorn producers

45. Give the appearance of

46. On one's ___ (alert)

47. ___ Butterworth's

48. Summer mo.

49. Queue after Q

50. "Boy, am ___ trouble!"

Solution on Page 281

ACROSS

1. Trade punches in training
5. Chew the fat
8. Make fun of
12. Greet from a distance
13. *Pulp Fiction* actress Thurman
14. Boast
15. Egyptian fertility goddess
16. Pistols, swords, etc.
18. Change residences
19. Dictionary entry: abbr.
20. Concludes
23. ___-off shotgun
28. Bridle part
31. The triple in a triple play
33. Couple
34. Develop over time
36. Lacking pigment
38. Thurmond of NBA fame
39. "___ Enchanted Evening" (*South Pacific* song)
41. ⅙ fl. oz.
42. Nose-in-the-air types
44. Dogs and cats
46. Poem of praise
48. Designer Chanel
52. Table tennis
57. Over again
58. Kuwaiti ruler
59. Closing letter
60. Volunteer St.
61. Stare
62. Make a mistake
63. Uses a sofa

DOWN

1. Sink's alternative
2. El ___, Tex.
3. Tel ___, Israel
4. View again
5. Astronaut Grissom
6. In the thick of
7. Wished
8. CEO's degree, maybe
9. Bruins great Bobby
10. "Overhead" engine part
11. Metric weights: abbr.
17. Gees' predecessors
21. Oct. follower
22. Membership fees
24. Police dept. alert
25. "But ___, there's more!"
26. German "one"
27. Plummet
28. Uncle ___ (rice brand)
29. "Terrible" czar
30. *The Wizard of Oz* dog
32. On the ___ wavelength (in accord)
35. Beirut's land: abbr.
37. Serve to be re-served

88

40. First game of the season

43. Soak up gravy

45. Skedaddles

47. Nod off

49. "That's ___ haven't heard"

50. Minimal money

51. Holds the title to

52. Where to hang one's hat

53. The Monkees' "___ Believer"

54. Little bite

55. Test for PhD wannabes

56. Eur. country

Solution on Page 281

ACROSS

1. *The Wizard of Oz* studio
4. Foldable beds
8. "Tasty!"
11. Spanish ones
13. Take ___ (respond to applause)
14. L–P filler
15. Speechless
16. "___, vidi, vici" (Caesar's boast)
17. Soup order
18. Curds and ___
20. Shuts with a bang
22. "Rise and ___!"
25. "Be Prepared" org.
26. Sally Field TV role
27. Boxer Tyson
30. Action word
34. Ornamental vase
35. Where hair roots grow
37. Chiang ___ (Thai city)
38. Huff and puff
40. Paper-and-string flier
41. Central
42. "Hurrah!"
44. Bonnie's partner in crime
46. Prodded, with "on"
49. Sushi bar soup
51. Myrna of the movies
52. Not closed
54. Social group
58. Apollo component
59. Sassy
60. Catcher's base
61. Many months: abbr.
62. DVR brand
63. Fed. purchasing group

DOWN

1. Britain's Queen ___
2. Bearded antelope
3. Bon ___ (witty remark)
4. Grotto
5. Comply with a command
6. Ship's weight unit
7. Holey cheese
8. 1978 hit with the lyric "You can get yourself clean, you can have a good meal"
9. E pluribus ___
10. Cleans the floor
12. Mended
19. Skirt lines
21. WC
22. Rudely overlook
23. Toss
24. ___ uncertain terms
25. Alternative to suspenders
28. Gross
29. China's Chiang ___-shek
31. Television award
32. Black Flag competitor
33. ___ one's time (wait)

90

36. Chest muscles, briefly

39. Zee preceder

43. Take in, as a stray

45. ___ Ness monster

46. ___ May of *The Beverly Hillbillies*

47. Ending for "theater" or "church"

48. Exercise establishments

49. Griffin who created *Jeopardy!*

50. Really liking, informally

53. Louvre Pyramid architect

55. Access the Internet, with "on"

56. Verbal stumbles

57. "Luck ___ Lady Tonight"

Solution on Page 282

ACROSS

1. Mouth-burning
4. Vermont harvest
7. Autobahn auto
10. Difficult burden
12. Zadora of *Butterfly*
13. Supreme Court justice ___ Bader Ginsburg
14. Stuff for stenos
16. Gomorrah gala
17. Biceps' place
18. Farm measures
19. Macintosh maker
22. Legendary actor Gregory
24. Hair removal brand
25. Fasten
28. Deep cut
29. '60s records
30. Indian flatbread
32. Musical Wonder
34. First 007 film
35. Sullen
36. Wimbledon court surface
37. Malign in print
40. Brazilian city
41. Sch. where John Wooden coached
42. *Daily Planet* reporter
47. "Neato!"
48. Check-cashing needs
49. Cafe au ___
50. UK country
51. When doubled, a nasty fly
52. Easy as ___

DOWN

1. Darlin'
2. Singer Yoko
3. King in a Steve Martin song
4. Computer junk mail
5. Assist
6. Partners for mas
7. Dueler with Hamilton
8. Homeowner's pymt.
9. Explanations
11. Make it official
13. Chuck Berry's genre
15. Post- opposite
18. Play a role
19. *Brokeback Mountain* director Lee
20. Pod veggies
21. Gnat or rat
22. Rock beater
23. UFO crew
26. Irene of *Fame*
27. ___ Christian Andersen
29. Actress Lucy
31. Refusals
33. TV control abbr.
36. Amer. soldiers

37. Clare Boothe ___

38. Clickable computer image

39. Internet journal

40. Move upward

42. Put a match to

43. ER drug disasters

44. Auto org.

45. Tip of a pen

46. And so forth

Solution on Page 282

ACROSS

1. Number between dos and cuatro
5. Prefix with dermal
8. Tom's ex before Nicole
12. Tamale wrapper
13. ___ out (deletes)
14. Height: abbr.
15. Beatles' meter maid
16. Poe story, "The ___ Heart"
18. Bi- halved
19. Zellweger of *Bridget Jones's Diary*
20. Gridiron gains: abbr.
21. Educator Horace
23. Spigot
25. Palestinian leader
27. Muscle twitches
31. ___ bat for
32. Castro's country
33. Come out
36. Off the right path
38. Fish with a charge
39. Flower holder
40. Former *Grand Ole Opry Live* network
43. Tied, as shoes
45. Groovy
48. Sudden and precipitous downturn
50. ___ Marie Presley
51. Not duped by
52. R followers
53. Bed with bars
54. "___ in Boots"
55. Hurricane hub
56. Declare untrue

DOWN

1. "No ___ traffic"
2. Make a mess of
3. Pre-repair job figure
4. Jamaican music
5. Scope
6. Hammer part
7. Archipelago parts
8. *When Harry ___ Sally…*
9. Faulkner's *As ___ Dying*
10. Merge
11. Singer Burl
17. Jump
19. Some genetic coding, for short
22. Prior to, old-style
24. International agreements
25. It goes before beauty, in a saying
26. CD-___
28. Can't-miss
29. Deg. for a corporate ladder climber
30. Put into words
34. Salon applications
35. Pass, as time
36. Street
37. Down in the dumps

40. 'Vette roof option

41. Half of Mork's farewell

42. Little lice

44. Part of NYC

46. X ___ xylophone

47. Newborn

49. Part of L.A.

50. Calc. display

Solution on Page 282

ACROSS

1. Get a blue ribbon
4. Spiced tea beverage
8. Part of IBM
12. Big commotion
13. Lasso material
14. Classic grape soda
15. Yang's complement
16. "Are you ___ out?"
17. Start an ovation
18. "Stainless" metal
20. Puts a stop to
21. Golf legend Sam
23. Caustic compounds
25. Short-tailed wildcat
26. Number in a quartet
27. Computer program, for short
30. Not outdoors
32. Lawrence of ___
34. Recolor
35. "No man ___ island"
37. E. ___ bacteria
38. Prefix with -pus
39. Tool with a bubble
40. Animal trap
43. ___ Island Red (chicken breed)
45. St. Paul's state
46. "Lemme ___!" (fightin' words)
47. Zest
50. "Go back" computer command
51. Bear whose porridge was too cold
52. Most common draw in Scrabble
53. Horse's stride
54. "The doctor ___"
55. Alternative to unleaded: abbr.

DOWN

1. Route
2. Exiled Amin
3. Hogwash
4. Sobbed
5. Sharpen, as a razor
6. Moon-landing program
7. Suffix with cash or cloth
8. Ancient Peruvians
9. *Ain't Misbehavin'* star Carter
10. ___ *Girl* (TV show)
11. They're kissable
19. Danny DeVito series
20. German mister
21. Lost traction
22. Big Apple address letters
24. Chinese currency
26. Suffix with Oktober
27. Better than average
28. Heap
29. Load for Jack and Jill
31. What high rollers roll
33. Scored 100 on an exam
36. Major blood vessels

1	2	3	■	4	5	6	7	■	8	9	10	11
12			■	13				■	14			
15			■	16				■	17			
■	■	18	19				■	20				
21	22				■	23	24			■	■	■
25				■	26			■	27	28	29
30			■	31		■	32		33			
34			■	35		36		■	37			
■	■	38				■	39				
40	41	42			■	43	44			■	■
45				■	46			■	47	48	49
50				■	51			■	52			
53				■	54			■	55			

38. "Ready ___, here…"

39. Fictional salesman Willy

40. Contentedly confident

41. Totenberg of NPR

42. "___ Love Her" (Beatles song)

44. Prefix meaning "half"

46. "___ making myself clear?"

48. U-turn from WSW

49. Cribbage board insert

Solution on Page 282

ACROSS

1. ___ Moines, IA
4. Bring to 212 degrees
8. Walk heavily
12. Kwik-E-Mart clerk on *The Simpsons*
13. Sore
14. Something to draw or toe
15. Large
16. Telescope user
18. Postal device
20. Bruce or Laura of Hollywood
21. High-___ monitor
22. Europe's "boot"
26. Confront
28. Office worker just for the day
31. "The Raven" writer
32. "I ___ Rock": Simon & Garfunkel
33. Mindful (of)
34. Educational org. founded in 1897
35. *Jeopardy!* whiz Jennings
36. Tight as a drum
37. "Hell ___ no fury…"
38. Apply, as pressure
40. Prickly husk
41. Prepares to fire
44. Nebraska metropolis
47. Cedes the crown
51. Word of advice
52. Committed perjury
53. Pants parts
54. Luau instrument, for short
55. Chops (off)
56. *Iliad* setting
57. Gender

DOWN

1. Applies lightly
2. Sweeping saga
3. Big crop in Hawaii
4. They're sometimes loaded on the field
5. Sept. follower
6. "If ___ a Hammer"
7. Ancient Greek instrument
8. What italics do
9. Designer Claiborne
10. Two halves
11. Aus. neighbor
17. Complain
19. Golfer Trevino
23. Equipment
24. Mississippi's Trent
25. "___, right!" ("I bet!")
26. Counterfeit
27. Nasdaq alternative
28. Bygone carrier
29. ___ Claire, Wis.
30. Mohawk-sporting actor
33. Basement's opposite

37. Sing without words

39. Fridge forays

40. Domineering

42. Beer component

43. Suffix with hip or quip

45. Take to the trail

46. Topmost point

47. Last word in the Pledge of Allegiance

48. Life story, for short

49. Bank acct. entry

50. Sense of self-importance

Solution on Page 283

ACROSS

1. "How do you like ___ apples?"
5. Car co. bought by Chrysler
8. Icky buildup
12. Banjo virtuoso Fleck
13. ___ Tse-tung
14. Despair's opposite
15. Tractor-trailer
16. Tavern
17. Pasadena's ___ Bowl
18. Scheme
19. Words in an analogy
21. Had a meal
24. Astound
28. Town shouters
31. Free-for-all
32. Fawn's mother
33. Jazz great Shaw
35. Pull
36. Face-to-face exams
38. Rodeo ropes
40. Buying binge
41. Network with annual awards
42. Chicago paper, briefly
45. Letters before gees
49. Witchy women
52. Adventure hero Swift
54. In ___ land (dreaming)
55. Sick as ___
56. "Not ___ shabby!"
57. Monorail unit
58. "Fly ___ the Moon"
59. Tiebreaker rounds: abbr.
60. Comic shrieks

DOWN

1. One of 16 in a cup: abbr.
2. Dog command
3. St. ___'s fire
4. Tiki bar order
5. Unit of current
6. Hawaii's "Valley Isle"
7. Corn throwaways
8. Auto trim
9. *Winnie-the-Pooh* baby
10. FedEx competitor
11. Barely passing grade
20. Least feral
22. Come-on
23. Screw things up
25. One above a tenor
26. Olympian ruler
27. Brain scan letters
28. Fortune 500 abbr.
29. Caboose position
30. Home of the NFL's Rams
32. Partners of don'ts
34. The Beatles' "___ the Walrus"
37. "Come on!"
39. Gracefully slender

43. "Sock ___ me!"

44. Cowboy's footwear

46. Price of a ride

47. Antiaircraft fire

48. ___ Club (discount chain)

49. Lunch meat

50. Suffix with lemon or orange

51. "I've ___ You Under My Skin"

53. Jan. and Feb.

Solution on Page 283

ACROSS

1. Fish propellers
5. Emergency PC key
8. Pub crawler
11. Judicial garb
12. Steffi of tennis
14. Dryly humorous
15. "Back ___ hour" (shop sign)
16. "You go, ___!"
17. Calligrapher's need
18. "___ Blinded Me with Science"
20. Walk softly
22. Ragged, as a garment
26. Letters on a chit
27. Suit ___ tee
28. Gin's partner
32. ___ pit (rock concert area)
34. Secret govt. group
36. ___ contendere
37. Protestant work ___
39. Britney Spears's "___ Slave 4 U"
41. Got hitched
42. *Wheel of Fortune* host
45. Sheep's coat
48. Like a fox
49. Debit color
50. Catches some rays
52. $20 bill dispensers
56. Ampersand
57. "Am ___ only one?"
58. Minnesota ballplayer
59. Something in Santa's bag
60. No spring chicken
61. Like takeout orders

DOWN

1. Sat. preceder
2. Particle with a charge
3. 76ers' org.
4. Touch, taste, or sight, e.g.
5. Incited
6. ___ Lanka
7. Magna ___
8. Loretta of *M*A*S*H*
9. Yes-___ question
10. Youngster
13. Bat one's eyelashes, say
19. Fedora, for one
21. Menial worker
22. Use a stopwatch
23. Owl sound
24. Frat recruiting event
25. Place to wash up
29. "___ lay me down…"
30. "Sorry if ___ you down"
31. Morse's creation
33. Bees' home
35. Piled up
38. Desert plants
40. Cobbler's tool

43. "Cool!"

44. Marriott competitor

45. *Animal House* grp.

46. Jay of late-night TV

47. Whirling water

51. Mighty Ducks' org.

53. Toddler's age

54. Russian fighter jet

55. Start with Cone or Cat

Solution on Page 283

ACROSS

1. Fast-paced jazz style
4. Jacuzzis
8. Roman sun god
11. Something to cram for
13. Cry from a sty
14. Weed-whacking tool
15. "Been there, ___ that"
16. Crumbly white cheese
17. Israeli gun
18. "There's gold in them ___ hills!"
20. Carries
22. Brag
25. Sonny's partner
27. Measure of resistance
28. "How do I love ___?"
30. Point on a wire fence
34. That man
35. Blue Ribbon brewer
37. Dove sound
38. Plant anchor
40. Carhop's carrier
41. Margarine container
42. "You never had ___ good!"
44. Nuisances
46. Hay machine
49. British weapon of WWII
51. Martian's craft, say
52. "Pay ___ mind"
54. Jockey's whip
58. Capote, to friends
59. Legume
60. Kind of jet
61. Letters of distress
62. "___, meeny, miney, mo"
63. Overseer of corp. accounts

DOWN

1. Sleeping spot
2. Losing tic-tac-toe line
3. Critique harshly
4. Couch potato's place
5. Remington Steele portrayer
6. Hill-building insect
7. Use Rollerblades
8. Open-and-___ case
9. Seep out
10. Hawaiian garlands
12. Big Apple baseball team
19. URL starter
21. Celestial sphere
22. Danish physicist Niels
23. Cleveland's state
24. *Guns* & ___ magazine
26. "___ real nowhere man…"
29. They may be tossed in the ring
31. *Macbeth* has five
32. Overwhelming defeat
33. Short hairdos
36. Use a Smith Corona

104

39. Deadlock

43. Cree or Crow

45. Abbr. on a business letter

46. "No ifs, ands, or ___"

47. Jackson 5 hairdo

48. Reed and Rawls

50. Theater award

53. Buttonless shirt

55. Kind of room or hall

56. Clumsy fellow

57. Golf teacher

Solution on Page 283

ACROSS

1. "What's ___ to like?"
4. Pigs ___ blanket
7. Like custard
11. Lumberjack's tool
12. Speaker's platform
14. TV handyman Bob
15. London's Big ___
16. Light, happy tune
17. "Janie's Got ___" (Aerosmith song)
18. Persevere
21. Ticked off but good
22. Pedal digit
23. Shoe fillers
25. ___ diem
26. AOL or MSN
29. K followers
30. Bea Arthur sitcom
32. ___ double take (show surprise)
33. Not home
34. Telepathic letters
35. Like *Playboy* models
36. Oft-swiveled joint
37. RN's touch
38. 1992 Dana Carvey film
43. Cat-o'-___-tails
44. ___ mein
45. Rainbow path
47. The Rolling Stones' "Time ___ My Side"
48. Mah-jongg piece
49. Cheerleader's cheer
50. Prefix meaning "six"
51. Gridiron org.
52. Mother sheep

DOWN

1. Catch, as a criminal
2. Yoke wearers
3. Slum dwelling
4. Ran in neutral
5. Neet rival
6. Needs medicine
7. Escape, as detection
8. "Thank Heaven for Little Girls" musical
9. Sticky stuff
10. ___ *Can Cook* (former cooking show)
13. Expressed
19. Tanner's tub
20. Days of ___ (long ago)
23. Showman Ziegfeld
24. Big bird
25. Young dog
26. "Oh, my!"
27. Chicago White ___
28. Salary
30. Lo ___ (noodle dish)
31. Facet

106

35. Camera initials

36. "Laughing" animal

37. Beach drier

38. All-knowing

39. Strong as ___

40. Much-kicked body part

41. Pack animal

42. Sketch

43. Fed. biomedical research agcy.

46. Guevara

Solution on Page 284

ACROSS

1. That guy's
4. *Ferris Bueller's Day* ___
7. Syllable before "la la"
10. "Your turn," to a walkie-talkie user
12. Museum-funding org.
13. Trendy
14. Combustible heap
15. "Stop the cameras!"
16. Bigger than big
17. Soviet ballistic missile
19. Smart-alecky
20. Walked with a purpose
23. Barracks bed
24. Pays attention to
25. Ended, as a subscription
28. "Yes," in Yokohama
29. Rebel Turner
30. Solemn promise
32. Get testy with
35. ___ de menthe
37. Wheel's edge
38. Whooping birds
39. Big bully
42. Lads
43. Floor coverings
44. Snorkeling accessory
45. Advanced degs.
49. With skill
50. Slip behind
51. When tripled, a *Seinfeld* catchphrase
52. Actress Susan
53. Land north of Mex.
54. U-turn from ENE

DOWN

1. Jump on one foot
2. Campus climber
3. Sunday talk: abbr.
4. Perfectly timed
5. Ongoing squabble
6. Jack Sprat's bane
7. Therefore
8. Fixes illegally
9. ___-deucey (card game)
11. Patch the lawn
13. Informal talks
18. Bank offerings, briefly
19. ___ up (absorb)
20. "Hush!"
21. Darjeeling and oolong
22. Harness strap
23. Feline
25. Back muscle, briefly
26. Divisible by two
27. Rotunda's crown
29. Swift boat vets' war
31. Craven of horror
33. ___-craftsy

34. Key lime, e.g.

35. Blubber

36. Grating, as a voice

38. Cuban line dance

39. Actor Pitt

40. Bumpkin

41. "The ___ Duckling"

42. Skewed view

44. Wintertime bug

46. Partner of hem

47. Cavity filler's deg.

48. Toothed tool

Solution on Page 284

ACROSS

1. Shamu or Willy
5. Harbor vessels
9. "I've got a mule, her name is ___"
12. Yank
13. "It's either you ___"
14. "Son ___ gun!"
15. Immediately, to a surgeon
16. Baptism, for one
17. Lighter and pen maker
18. Trousers
20. Sticky stuff
22. Main order in a restaurant
24. Director Brooks
25. Blue-ribbon position
26. Salad ingredient
29. Transcript stat
30. Antonym's antonym: abbr.
31. Tiny amount
33. Globe or ball
36. String quartet member
38. Little ___ (tots)
39. Brought in, as a salary
40. ___ cum laude
43. Tippy craft
44. GI entertainment sponsor
45. Super Mario ___
47. "Nothing," in Spain
50. "Yes" signal
51. Erie or Huron
52. Jim Croce's "___ a Name"
53. Maybes
54. Sized up visually
55. Boston hoopster, for short

DOWN

1. Photo ___ (picture-taking times)
2. Oxcart's track
3. Nonsense
4. Church platforms
5. Rich pastry
6. Literary Leon
7. Intl. clock standard
8. Oozed
9. Bawls
10. Throw ___ (get angry)
11. Valentine decoration
19. Badminton divider
21. MacGraw of *Love Story*
22. Three after D
23. Puppy bites
24. "You da ___!"
26. Whiskey variety
27. Caveman's era
28. ___ and hearty
30. Grads-to-be: abbr.
32. "Dear old" fellow
34. Barbarian
35. Allow
36. Mover's vehicle

37. Humorously sarcastic

39. Let up

40. City bond, for short

41. ___ now (immediately)

42. Mount Olympus dwellers

43. Pepsi competitor

46. Bit of sunshine

48. Amer. currency

49. Lawyer: abbr.

Solution on Page 284

ACROSS

1. Air passage
5. Poehler of *SNL*
8. ___ *Angel* (Mae West film)
12. "___ be wrong, but…"
13. Feathered stole
14. Genesis son
15. Jamie of *M*A*S*H*
16. ___ Kippur
17. Tasting of wood, as some wines
18. Eeyore is one
20. Santa Fe's st.
21. Makes amends
24. Men and boys
26. Terre ___, Indiana
27. Golf target
28. Day- ___: pigment brand
31. Gives the green light
32. Milan's La ___
34. Hit on the knuckles
35. "You ain't seen nothin' ___!"
36. Rat-a-___ (drum sound)
37. Confiscate
39. "Right in the kisser!" preceder
40. A, B, or C
41. Viral video, e.g.
44. Cigarette's end
45. Cut from the staff
46. *Larry King Live* channel
48. Fraction of a foot
52. ___ monster (large lizard)
53. Use a shovel
54. Crime chief
55. "___ cost you!"
56. Devon river
57. Like a bug in a rug

DOWN

1. "What's the ___?" ("Who cares?")
2. Actress Thurman
3. ___ *and Driver* (popular magazine)
4. Despot
5. Yawning gulf
6. Cow's sound
7. Thanksgiving side dish
8. Computer symbols
9. "Just the facts, ___"
10. Reebok rival
11. Black gemstone
19. Takes care of
21. Seaman's shout
22. "___ it or leave it!"
23. Topple from power
24. Computer in *2001*
25. Cleans the chalkboard
27. Butter serving
28. Abrasive particles
29. Take it easy
30. 0 on a phone: abbr.
33. Crow's cry

Puzzle 52

38. Moral principles
39. Piano part
40. Actress Jessica
41. Biblical wise men
42. Leave the stage
43. Pell-___
46. Three after B
47. Put the kibosh on
49. Indian bread
50. PC's "brain"
51. Take more than one's share of

Solution on Page 284

ACROSS

1. U-turn from NNE
4. Brother of George W.
7. Crooner Crosby
11. Melville hero
13. Brian of rock music
14. Writing on the wall
15. Created
16. Hesitation sounds
17. "Pet" that's a plant
18. Home run king Hank
20. Young horse
21. Twirls
24. Wingless parasites
26. Clark's exploring partner
27. "Well, ___-di-dah!"
28. Computer screen, for short
31. Parisian goodbye
32. 1950's candidate Stevenson
34. Actor Diesel
35. "Tell ___ story"
38. Push roughly
39. Use a Kindle, say
40. ___ Tots
41. Colt's mother
44. Rodeo performer
46. ___ a Teenage Werewolf
47. Prefix with cycle
48. Baseball glove
52. Pre-Easter season
53. Half a laugh
54. Greenish blue
55. Gambler's numbers
56. Tally (up)
57. "Wait a ___!"

DOWN

1. Patriotic uncle
2. Al Green's "___-La-La"
3. Roll of dough
4. Express derision
5. Sign up
6. Neighbor of Croatia
7. Italian bowling game
8. "If you ask me," in textspeak
9. Diamond or Sedaka
10. Pesky flying insect
12. ___ Babies
19. Presuppose
21. Serb or Croat
22. Mani-___
23. "Heads ___, tails you lose"
25. Pure as the driven snow
28. Arterial blockage
29. Great review
30. Layer of a wedding cake
33. TV's ___ and Greg
36. Singer Kitt
37. Cherished
39. Catches one's breath

41. Venus de ___

42. Impressed deeply

43. McNally's partner

45. ___ Piper

49. Stanford-Binet nos.

50. Day of the wk.

51. Between tic and toe

Solution on Page 285

ACROSS

1. Study hard and fast
5. Run-of-the-mill: abbr.
8. Murders, mob-style
12. Vatican VIP
13. Flying geese formation
14. Advertising award
15. Alternatives to pumpernickels
16. Audiologist's concern
17. Neat
18. Mar. follower
20. Makes very happy
22. Supervisors
25. It's north of Okla.
26. UCLA rival
27. Keanu's *The Matrix* role
29. First showing
33. Govt. mortgage provider
34. Sullivan and Harris
36. "Can ___ now?"
37. Language of Iran
40. Temperature abbr.
42. Notwithstanding that, briefly
43. New Deal program, for short
45. Motionless
47. Drive-in feature
50. Mauna ___ volcano
51. Zen riddle
52. Call ___ day (retire)
54. Pig in the movies

58. "___ Excited" (Pointer Sisters hit)
59. Possess
60. High-fiber food
61. Energizes, with "up"
62. ___-picker (overly critical one)
63. "___ first you don't succeed…"

DOWN

1. Lifeguard's skill, for short
2. Orbison who sang "Only the Lonely"
3. King Kong, notably
4. Flat-topped hills
5. Supervise
6. New Deal agcy.
7. Bo of "10"
8. Gas number
9. Dart about
10. Bona ___ (authentic)
11. Beans used for tofu
19. Signer's need
21. Young chap
22. Polish, as shoes
23. Worker protection org.
24. Surgery memento
28. Strange
30. Angler's quest
31. Cries of aversion
32. Choo-choo's sound
35. Caulking

38. Dictation takers

39. "___ Gotta Be Me" (Sammy Davis Jr. song)

41. Powerful Pontiac

44. Negatively charged particle

46. Synagogue leader

47. Omit

48. "O ___, All Ye Faithful"

49. Hoarse voice

53. ___-night doubleheader

55. Dog's bark

56. Bleat

57. Sinus doc

Solution on Page 285

ACROSS

1. Surfer's need
6. Little rascal
9. Banquet hosts: abbr.
12. Title holder
13. Gloppy stuff
14. "See ___ care!"
15. Al ___ (pasta style)
16. "C'___ la vie!"
17. Oui's opposite
18. In the company of
20. Smooch
21. Stick (out)
24. Painter Rivera
26. Naval letters
27. In great shape
28. "It's ___ a day's work"
32. Approached
34. Emotional shock
35. Swashbuckling Flynn
36. Abrade
37. Newsstand buy, for short
38. In the box and ready to hit
40. Dell or Toshiba products, for short
41. Skipped town
44. Put on the line
46. Start of the Lord's Prayer
47. Is afflicted with
48. Twisted to one side
53. Nonprofit's URL ending
54. Night before a holiday
55. L.L.Bean's home
56. Bout ender, briefly
57. "Da Ya Think I'm Sexy?" singer Stewart
58. Tequila plant

DOWN

1. Physique, informally
2. Be indebted to
3. Andy's raggedy pal
4. On a pension: abbr.
5. Sketched
6. "Aha!"
7. Israeli leader Dayan
8. Money on a poker table
9. ___ Cooper (popular car)
10. Corp. money managers
11. Confessional list
19. "___ it my way"
20. Soft drink nut
21. Father's Day month
22. ___-friendly
23. Old Russian royal
25. Attire
27. Hat fabric
29. "One ___ or two?"
30. Apple product
31. Old horses
33. Highway

118

34. King ___ tomb

36. Saw through childhood

39. "Well done!"

41. ___ the bill: pay

42. Lie in wait

43. Logician's "therefore"

45. ___ Sutra

47. ___ Royal Highness

49. Sink in the middle

50. Korean automaker

51. Ltr. carrier

52. Pint-sized

Solution on Page 285

ACROSS

1. Little troublemakers
5. NJ neighbor
8. On ___ streak (winning)
12. Goalie's goal
13. Affirmative at sea
14. ___-pedi
15. Abbr. before a name on an envelope
16. Gp. pursuing pushers
17. Radar image
18. Retort to "Are not!"
20. Casino machines
21. Hindu social division
24. Beat a retreat
26. Like smooth-running machines
27. ___ Bo (exercise system)
28. When doubled, a dance
31. ___ first-name basis
32. Sighing sounds
33. Need a doctor's care
34. Gas additive letters
35. Feel sorry about
36. Takes an apartment
38. Labels
39. "Am not!" reply
40. In flames
43. "So long!"
45. Connection point
46. ___ mot (witticism)
47. Counterfeit

51. Cabbage's kin
52. Sea eagle
53. Austen novel made into a 1996 movie
54. Tan and Irving
55. Ambulance letters
56. Shower affection (on)

DOWN

1. "A rose ___ rose…"
2. Floor covering
3. Lowest army rank: abbr.
4. 100-member group
5. Family men
6. Cyclonic center
7. Thompson of *Back to the Future*
8. Mosey along
9. Angel topper
10. Words after step or sleep
11. Gratuities
19. Size between sm. and lge.
20. View
21. Dove sounds
22. "Say it ___ so!"
23. Hockey shot
25. ___ Cruces, NM
28. Charlie Chaplin prop
29. Top 40 songs
30. "And another thing…"
32. Sept. preceder
35. *Norma* ___ (Field film)

36. Hamelin pest
37. Rubbed out
38. Elm and oak
40. "Puppy Love" singer Paul
41. Lather
42. Without purpose
44. Raggedy dolls

46. Spelling contest
48. Medical care grp.
49. Quantity: abbr.
50. Fannie ___ (federal mortgage agency)

Solution on Page 285

ACROSS

1. Organs with drums
5. Lifeless
9. Potter pal Weasley
12. Shoelace snarl
13. Bush advisor Karl
14. Literary collection
15. Startling revelation
17. Pol. party
18. ___ *Miserables*
19. Choirs may stand on them
21. Small bays
24. Super Bowl stats
25. *60 Minutes* pundit Andy
26. Puts in the mail
29. Give it ___ (attempt to do)
30. Letters before a pseudonym
32. Petty quarrels
36. Actor Omar
39. Philosopher ___ Tzu
40. Bemoan
41. To the rear, on a ship
44. "Telephone Line" rock grp.
45. Novelist Tolstoy
46. Former Secretary of State
    Albright
51. Opposite of max.
52. At the pinnacle of
53. ___-a-brac
54. Deflation sound
55. Trash holders
56. "It should come ___ surprise"

DOWN

1. ___ out an existence
2. "___ takers?"
3. Salmon eggs
4. Like some kisses and bases
5. Fancy, as clothes
6. Many millennia
7. Turns away
8. Ridicule
9. All the ___ (wildly popular)
10. ___ about (roughly)
11. Tots' rests
16. St. ___ (spring break spot)
20. W-2 ID
21. Roth ___ (investment choice)
22. Holiday drinks
23. Aerobatic maneuver
27. Madonna's *Truth or* ___
28. Birthday suit
31. Back at sea
33. Pint at a pub
34. Airport surface
35. Beethoven's "Moonlight ___"
36. Nods off
37. Room connector
38. One-celled protozoan
41. Donations for the poor

122

42. Cinco follower

43. Heaps

47. ___ *Quixote*

48. Form 1040 org.

49. Diarist Anais

50. ___-friendly (green)

Solution on Page 286

ACROSS

1. Bear's abode
4. Scuba tank supply
7. Really hate
12. Toon pal of Stimpy
13. "One," in Madrid
14. Davis of *A League of Their Own*
15. Becomes enraged
17. Get through to
18. Part of a Dracula costume
19. Actor Zimbalist Jr.
20. Pate de ___ gras
23. "___ honest with you…"
25. Tehran native
27. Pathetically inept person
32. Light-sensitive eye part
34. *A Streetcar Named Desire* woman
35. "College" member who votes for president
37. Perfectly pitched
38. ___ out a living (barely got by)
40. Umpire's call
41. Happen
45. "Elder" or "Younger" Roman statesman
47. Sedan alternative
48. Tipped off
52. Leans to one side
53. "No way, laddie!"
54. "Now ___ theater near you!"
55. Parcel out
56. Comic Conway
57. Feb. preceder

DOWN

1. Salk and Pepper: abbr.
2. Wide shoe spec
3. SSW's reverse
4. Radiant glow
5. Hapless
6. Cowboy contests
7. Accepted
8. Hamburger meat
9. "Now ___ this!"
10. Fairy tale's first word
11. Chicago mayor Emanuel
16. Eye-pleasing, as a view
20. Cannoneer's command
21. Pitcher Hershiser
22. "Must've been something ___"
24. Undergrad degs.
26. Bank accrual
28. Motion detector, e.g.
29. ___-Seltzer (antacid brand)
30. First symbol on a musical staff
31. Danny of *White Christmas*
33. Fine
36. Take back, as testimony
39. The ___ Lama
41. Tetra- doubled

42. Slinky's shape
43. Select
44. "I've had it ___ here!"
46. Abound (with)
49. ___ Mahal
50. When a plane is due in: abbr.
51. Rather of news

Solution on Page 286

ACROSS

1. Blast furnace by-product
5. Some med. scans
9. Hoover's org.
12. Gomer of TV
13. Lee or Grant: abbr.
14. Hockey Hall of Famer Bobby
15. Affirmative votes
16. Rice-A-___
17. Comics shriek
18. "___ better to have loved and lost…"
20. Spanish houses
22. Secret agents
25. High school sci. course
27. Gore and Green
28. Joke response
30. St. Louis attraction
34. Sha ___ (doo-wop group)
36. Propel a dinghy
37. Explorer of kids' TV
38. Old Pontiacs
39. ___ Major (Great Bear)
41. Mooch, as a cigarette
42. Sharp part of a knife
44. Prescribed amounts
46. Armistice
49. Benjamin Hoff's The ___ of Pooh
50. ThinkPad maker
51. Sky-colored
54. Marcel Marceau, e.g.

58. Potato chip accompaniment
59. Bird with a forked tail
60. Strait-laced
61. Snaky curve
62. River deposit
63. Furnace output

DOWN

1. Le Carré character
2. Soapmaker's solution
3. Turkey ___ king
4. *Beau* ___ (Gary Cooper classic)
5. Baseball bosses: abbr.
6. Rock's ___ Speedwagon
7. Rural stopover
8. It's a piece of cake
9. Enemies
10. La ___ Tar Pits
11. Irritates
19. Relative of -esque
21. *Diary of ___ Housewife*
22. Crooned
23. Real-estate map
24. "Money ___ object"
25. Allowance-earning task, perhaps
26. Hems and ___
29. Snug as a bug in ___
31. Steals from
32. Rock band Motley ___
33. Radio operators

35. "Hold on ___!"

40. Dentists' org.

43. Financial obligations

45. Vitality

46. Ocean's motion

47. Stats for sluggers

48. Strike callers

49. Circus enclosure

52. Hawaiian wreath

53. WWW address

55. Bitter feeling

56. Hamm of soccer fame

57. Ambulance worker, for short

Solution on Page 286

ACROSS

1. Drags along
5. Not that
9. Preschooler
12. "___ just me, or…"
13. Puerto ___
14. "…cup ___ cone?"
15. Anti-fur org.
16. Quick joke
18. Dull impact sound
20. Parts of molecules
21. Souvenir garment
24. Chem. or bio.
25. Grand stories
26. Teeter-totters
30. Trucker's tractor trailer
31. "___ Your Head on My Shoulder"
32. Cartographer's product
33. Jock
36. Egyptian capital
38. Small batteries
39. 14-line poem
40. ___ Ababa, Ethiopia
43. Elvis moved his, famously
44. Walked unsteadily
46. ___ Harry Met Sally…
50. Cry after an epiphany
51. Trout tempter
52. Cyberauction site
53. Indy 500 month
54. Snooty sort
55. Univ. military program

DOWN

1. Collagen injection site
2. Deplete, with "up"
3. "Scram, varmint!"
4. Radio broadcast interference
5. Brook fish
6. Posterior
7. Freezer trayful
8. Comfort
9. Up ___ good
10. City near Provo
11. ___ and feathers
17. "How sweet ___!"
19. Mins. add up to them
21. Trillion: prefix
22. ___ and polish
23. Way up there
24. "Ready, ___, go!"
26. Haul into court
27. Despot Idi ___
28. Suffix with hard or soft
29. "See ___ run"
31. Qt. halves
34. ___-back (relaxed)
35. Artists' stands
36. Officer of the peace
37. "Is that your final ___?"

128

39. Lesser-played half of a 45

40. Noted rib donor

41. Capital of Qatar

42. June 6, 1944

43. Rescuer, to a rescuee

45. Sprint

47. Cable movie channel

48. Chow down

49. Big Apple inits.

Solution on Page 286

ACROSS

1. Shoulder enhancer
4. Contemptible fellow
7. Modifying wd.
10. Animal with a beard
12. His Master's Voice company
13. What V-J Day ended
14. Annually published fact books
16. ___ Kong (Chinese port)
17. Fuzzy green fruit
18. Thaws
19. Urge
22. ___ John letter
24. Free of clutter
25. Gist
29. Poland's Walesa
30. Lorne Michaels show
31. James Brown's genre
32. Take a shot at
34. Word with hay or live
35. Complain
36. Sultan's wives
37. Face-valued, as stocks
40. Projection room spool
42. "___, ma! No hands!"
43. Like a pendulum's swing
47. Drill a hole
48. Response to a ques.
49. Lena or Ken of film
50. Supermodel Carol
51. Put money (on)
52. Appropriate

DOWN

1. Ryder Cup org.
2. Yahoo! alternative
3. Reservoir creator
4. Stick in one's ___ (rankle)
5. Klutzy
6. ___ *Boot* (1981 war film)
7. Barracks no-show
8. By ___ of (owing to)
9. Irish dances
11. Be extraordinary
13. Popular seek-and-find series
15. Not even one
18. Barker and Bell
19. *To Live and Die* ___
20. Track and field contest
21. Hostilities ender
23. Subj. for some immigrants
26. Film ___ (movie genre)
27. Heal
28. Grades 1–6: abbr.
30. Apr. season
33. Dent or scratch
36. Biddy
37. *Dark Angel* star Jessica
38. Ax or awl
39. Dessert wine

130

41. Steinbeck's ___ of Eden

43. It's run up and then settled

44. EPCOT's home

45. Headstone letters

46. It's west of Que.

Solution on Page 287

ACROSS

1. It's scanned at checkout: abbr.
4. ___-Tac-Dough
7. Wet ground
10. Dollop
12. University web address suffix
13. ___ song (cheaply)
14. 3-D picture
16. Dice throw
17. 12, on a sundial
18. Sloppy
19. One with a halo
22. Feathered friend
24. Wall Street pessimist
25. Hard Italian cheese
28. Totals
29. "It's c-c-cold!"
30. Solar-system centers
32. Iran's capital
34. Calc prerequisite
35. Cries at fireworks
36. Tease
37. Polo or tee
40. "The Sweetheart of Sigma ___"
41. Southpaw's side
42. Follow
47. Clodhoppers
48. Perjure oneself
49. Covetousness
50. Tissue layer
51. Sunday seat
52. Alternate to dial-up, for short

DOWN

1. Sound of discomfort
2. Mahmoud Abbas's grp.
3. Rank above maj.
4. Hatcher or Garr
5. Ore-___ (frozen food brand)
6. Summa ___ laude
7. Dairy farm sounds
8. Internet addresses
9. Tyne of *Cagney & Lacey*
11. Alternative to briefs
13. Epitome of class in dance
15. ___ Gerard (Buck Rogers portrayer)
18. Med. scan
19. Stomach muscles
20. Neither masc. nor fem.
21. *The Pajama ___*, Doris Day film
22. Buildings with lofts
23. Jerusalem is its cap.
26. Wise advisor
27. "What's going ___ there?"
29. Ebenezer's exclamation
31. Certain NCO
33. Start to smell, maybe
36. Fill in ___ blank
37. Sty food

38. Make well

39. In doubt

40. Not just swallow whole

42. The Matterhorn, for one

43. Six-sided roller

44. What boring things never seem to do

45. Tubes

46. Olive in the comics

Solution on Page 287

ACROSS

1. Massages
5. On the ___ (fleeing)
8. "Time ___ the essence"
12. Octagonal street sign
13. Audition, with "out"
14. Knocker's place
15. Barn topper
16. Morse code component
17. Dr. Seuss's *Horton Hears ___!*
18. Cry of relief
19. "Not gonna happen"
21. Omen
24. Junction points
28. Docs, for short
31. Beatty of *Deliverance*
32. Immature insect
33. Give a new title to
35. Thin layer of wood
36. Singer Baker
37. Family member, informally
38. Type
39. March 17 honoree, for short
40. Flat-topped mountain
42. Plastic building block
44. Broadway offering
48. Yodel's comeback
51. Soft toss
53. Fish in a melt
54. San ___ Obispo, Calif.
55. Needing no prescription: abbr.
56. War partner
57. Classic sneakers
58. Advanced degree: abbr.
59. Purchases

DOWN

1. Invitation letters
2. Salt Lake City's home
3. Dog's treat
4. Gushes forth
5. Inc., in Britain
6. In the neighborhood
7. Legendary story
8. Man from Boise
9. Scatter, as seeds
10. "Wow!"
11. To's opposite
20. Except if
22. Cell occupant
23. "___ whiz!"
25. Eins + zwei
26. Stuntman Knievel
27. *Cutty ___* (historic ship)
28. Mardi ___
29. Confined, with "up"
30. Tiny scissor cut
34. Baffled
35. Go head to head
37. Silky

134

41. Take ___ at (try)

43. Unappetizing food

45. Streaming video giant

46. Nothing more than

47. ___ and Means Committee

48. Caribou cousin

49. Actor's prompt

50. Kept out of sight

52. String after A

Solution on Page 287

ACROSS

1. Solemn wedding words
4. Broad bean
8. Captain Morgan's drink
11. Arrests
13. Take down ___ (demote)
14. NYSE debut
15. Lit ___ (English major's class)
16. Gorilla researcher Fossey
17. Noticeable opening
18. Poker-pot starters
20. Raise
22. Fem. opposite
24. Repartee
25. Agt.'s take
28. "___ on truckin'"
30. Tennis champ Bjorn
33. Inspire, as curiosity
35. Nevertheless
37. ___ of the Flies
38. Welles role
40. "___ be an honor"
41. Lean-___ (sheds)
43. "That was ___ ..."
45. Distinguished
48. "Poison" shrub
52. Animation unit
53. Ear-busting
55. Spy ___ Hari
56. ___ and vinegar
57. Maître d's handout
58. Very dry, as wine
59. Hunters' org.
60. Hasn't ___ to stand on
61. Network with an eye logo

DOWN

1. Peruvian of yore
2. "Phooey!"
3. Memorial news item
4. Craze
5. For each
6. Calf meat
7. Vice President Spiro
8. Tubular pasta
9. ___ the crack of dawn
10. Sulk
12. Flower's support
19. ___ Fifth Avenue
21. Slangy feeling
23. Hide's partner
25. Chum
26. ___-Magnon (early human)
27. Mexican food staple
29. Phnom ___, Cambodia
31. Q–U connector
32. "In ___ We Trust"
34. Japanese soup noodles
36. Geese formations
39. Bring into harmony

136

Puzzle 64

42. 1965 Alabama march site
44. Feeling no pain
45. Greenspan's subj.
46. Israel's Golda
47. Yuletide song
49. Singer Anthony
50. "Three men in ___"
51. Meowers
54. Used a shovel

Solution on Page 287

ACROSS

1. Lad
4. No. on a bank statement
8. Pharmaceutical watchdog grp.
11. Bud
12. "Pants on fire" fellow
13. Co. honchos
14. Letters after a proof
15. Indonesian island
16. "What the ___!"
17. Intent look
19. Lose luster
21. Two-by-two vessel
23. Hungarian composer Franz
26. Blew, as a volcano
30. Ringo of the Beatles
32. *Annie Get Your ___*
33. Itching desire
35. Election Day mo.
36. "Dig?"
39. Fixes securely
42. Philanthropist
44. "That's a laugh!"
45. Newspaper opinion piece
47. Gambler's lady?
50. "I have ___ good authority"
53. Art ___ (1920s–1930s style)
55. Old horse
57. Sidewalk eatery
58. "___ Fire" (Springsteen hit)
59. Underwire garment
60. Battleship score
61. Lowers, as a light
62. Playfully shy

DOWN

1. Grilling, for short
2. State north of Calif.
3. Luke Skywalker's mentor
4. London's Royal ___ Hall
5. Undercover org.
6. Baby bovine
7. Courtroom event
8. Finder's charge
9. Holliday of the Old West
10. "Don't ___, don't tell"
13. Where the toys are
18. Nuke
20. Talk smack about
22. ___ Largo
24. Western writer Grey
25. 1982 Disney film starring Jeff Bridges
26. Sunny-side up item
27. Had misgivings about
28. "Do ___ others, then run": Benny Hill
29. Rock's ___ Leppard
31. Winnebagos, briefly
34. Slangy denial

138

37. Hole ___ (golfer's dream)
38. Go one better than
40. Beauty parlors
41. Turkey Day day: abbr.
43. Changed the decor of
46. Actress Moore
48. Business TV channel

49. Corn syrup brand
50. "___ liebe dich"
51. Mai ___ (rum-based beverage)
52. Frequently, to bards
54. Dot-___ (Internet company)
56. Like old Paree

Solution on Page 288

ACROSS

1. ___ of Iran
5. German "eight"
9. Suffix with Benedict
12. Promo recording
13. Person of action
14. Dustcloth
15. "Should that be true…"
16. She had a soft bed
18. ___ fixe (menu notation)
20. Explorer ___ de Leon
21. Beverage chest
24. Aug. follower
25. "___, Martin and John"
27. Last year of the third century
28. Letter after chi
29. Medicinal plants
31. Top poker card
34. Wane
36. Supreme ruler
38. Acting Anderson
40. Monkey treat
41. In a fitting manner
43. Cobra's weapon
44. Death Valley is below it
46. Imitated
50. Explosive stuff
51. Actor Neeson
52. Precious metal
53. Reverse of NNW
54. ___ down (frisks)
55. Tweak, as text

DOWN

1. High-tech weapons prog.
2. *Playboy* Hugh, familiarly
3. Morning hrs.
4. Fanfare
5. Head of a fleet
6. Try to persuade
7. Garment bottom
8. Sting operation, e.g.
9. "Flashdance…What a Feeling" singer
10. Civil rights org.
11. Wading bird
17. Popular pear
19. Get-well program
21. ___ and gown
22. Out of date: abbr.
23. Get one's bearings
26. *The Simpsons* bartender
27. Senate broadcaster
30. Mummifies
32. One side of an issue
33. Cenozoic or Mesozoic
35. List of charges
37. Take on
38. Endures
39. Begins on Broadway

42. Kennel cry
43. Heroic deed
45. By means of
47. Pea container
48. ___ Lilly & Co.
49. Chemical used to fight malaria

Solution on Page 288

ACROSS

1. "Either he goes ___ go!"
4. Sound of distress
8. Coll. or univ.
11. Trips around the track
13. "… ___ I've been told"
14. *Hollywood Squares* win
15. Sudden wind
16. Thai currency
17. Purchase
18. Not silently
20. Middle grade
21. Place to get a mud bath
22. Rotary phone feature
24. Fast plane: abbr.
26. "I do"
29. Crossed (out)
31. Lounge
34. Opposed (to)
36. Loves to pieces
38. German philosopher Immanuel
39. Small, medium, or large
41. Since 1/1, to a CPA
42. Chairman pro ___
44. Attorney General Janet
46. Knock the socks off of
48. ___ Z (you name it)
50. Jazz singer Vaughan
54. ___ Tin Tin (TV dog)
55. Crips or Bloods
57. "Oompah" instrument
58. Corp. abbr.
59. Light bulb, in cartoons
60. Estate receiver
61. Last letter
62. Sagan or Sandburg
63. Pt. of EST

DOWN

1. Olympic gymnast Korbut
2. Julia of *The Addams Family*
3. ___ facto
4. Rioting group
5. Soothsayer
6. Tennis champ Arthur
7. Student's jottings
8. Tale of woe
9. ___ d'etat
10. Georgetown athlete
12. Variety of poker
19. ___ laughing (cracks up)
23. Lumberjacks' tools
25. ___-mo
26. Tibetan ox
27. Zsa Zsa's sister
28. Convicted criminal's punishment
30. Knock for a loop
32. "___ there be light"
33. "Turn on, tune in, drop out" drug
35. 66, e.g.: abbr.

37. Bears' lairs
40. Laundry worker
43. Like Mozart's flute
45. Swearing-in statement
46. NM neighbor
47. Chianti or Chablis
49. "I did it!"

51. Laments
52. Just slightly
53. Rocklike
56. Guy's counterpart

Solution on Page 288

ACROSS

1. City WSW of Phoenix
5. Violinists' needs
9. UK leaders
12. Like two peas in ___
13. Banister
14. Jr.'s son
15. ___ colada (rum cocktail)
16. Chichen ___ (Mayan ruins)
17. CIA Cold War counterpart
18. Coll. senior's test
20. "God ___ America"
22. "Me and Bobby ___"
25. "How ___ to know?"
27. Rowing need
28. Military stronghold
30. Sportscaster Albert
34. Barbershop request
36. "___ the land of the free…"
37. Scott of *Charles in Charge*
38. Overpublicize
39. Picks up the tab
41. "Good" cholesterol, briefly
42. "Slipped" backbone part
44. Item of value
46. Chubby Checker's dance
49. Broadcast regulatory org.
50. Order to a firing squad
51. Prefix meaning "same"
54. Meat package letters
58. Book balancer, briefly
59. "___ the word!"
60. *The Simpsons* son
61. Put a spell on
62. Frosh, next year
63. *Beverly Hills Cop* character Foley

DOWN

1. Bark sharply
2. News initials
3. Tue. preceder
4. Wise saying
5. Runny French cheese
6. Feed seed
7. *The* ___ (Diana Ross musical)
8. Thick slices
9. Toll road
10. Russian fighter jets
11. Bro and sis
19. Whistleblower on a court
21. An arm or a leg
22. One drawn to a flame
23. Actor Grant
24. Hold
25. Inflict, as havoc
26. Give it ___ (attempt)
29. "I goofed"
31. Sounds of relief
32. Ticket to ___
33. Battery unit

Puzzle 68

35. Prescriptions, for short
40. Kangaroo pouch
43. Agenda details
45. Diver's gear
46. RPM indicator
47. Dry dishes
48. Giant screen film format
49. Guppy or grouper
52. Quid pro ___
53. Strike caller
55. Clinton's instrument
56. "Dr." with Grammys
57. US/Eur. divider

Solution on Page 288

ACROSS

1. Popular cooking spray
4. Several
8. Jittery
12. High ___ kite
13. All used up
14. Spanish surrealist Joan
15. Drunk's sound
16. Bausch & ___ (lens maker)
17. Library volume
18. Battery terminal
20. Cusp
21. Toss
23. Slide on ice
25. Ukraine's capital
26. "___ there?" (part of a knock-knock joke)
27. "___ death do us part"
30. Richly decorated
32. Maple leaf land
34. Where the buoys are
35. Launder
37. Grp. that has energy users over a barrel?
38. Soil
39. Flowery verse
40. Map within a map
43. Paradises
45. Cowgirl Evans
46. Englishman, for short
47. ___ Lizzie (Model T)
50. Apple MP3 player
51. Cop's route
52. Cleanup hitter's stat
53. Chews the fat
54. Snug and warm
55. "Uh-huh"

DOWN

1. Oom-___ band
2. "___ always say…"
3. Dance craze of the '90s
4. Radiant
5. Chow
6. Catch, as in a net
7. Spider's creation
8. Fix firmly
9. Christian in fashion
10. Sailor's rum drink
11. Oxen's harness
19. Bossa ___
20. Mastercard alternative
21. Ring decisions, for short
22. Give the job to
24. Former New York mayor Ed
26. Dress in
27. Classic Carole King album
28. ___ of March
29. Like a doily
31. Ninny

146

33. Common lunchtime

36. Not mono

38. Owners' documents

39. Trivial

40. "Got it, man"

41. California wine valley

42. Oscar Madison, for one

44. Actress Cameron

46. UK channel

48. "Where would ___ without you?"

49. Small bite

Solution on Page 289

ACROSS

1. Tick off
4. "Was ___ blame?"
7. Crunchy sandwiches, for short
11. "___ make myself clear?"
12. Rolling stones lack it
14. Cousin of an onion
15. "Wise" bird
16. Mope
17. Forever and ___
18. ___ *Weapon* (Mel Gibson film)
20. Meditation sounds
22. Raised railways
23. Compass part
27. Barton of the American Red Cross
30. Morning dampness
31. Nay canceler
32. Belonging to you and me
33. IHOP beverages
34. *Porgy and* ___
35. Studio once controlled by Howard Hughes
36. ___ *Doubtfire*
37. Delicious
38. Signify
40. Precious stone
41. Chow mein additive
42. *Citizen Kane*'s real-life model
46. Netanyahu, familiarly
49. In the blink ___ eye
51. Bullfight bravo
52. ___ above (better than)
53. Women in habits
54. Bygone Russian space station
55. Courage, informally
56. Aye's opposite
57. Cash dispenser, briefly

DOWN

1. Person on a pedestal
2. Investment firm T. ___ Price
3. Bagpiper's wear
4. African antelope
5. Hammer and sickle, e.g.
6. Columbus campus initials
7. Nonchalant
8. Paved the way
9. Oolong or pekoe
10. Shade of blue
13. Gems
19. Woman's pronoun
21. Cat call
24. Henna and others
25. "... ___ ye be judged"
26. Not hard
27. Parachute part
28. One of the Gospels
29. Schoenberg opera *Moses und* ___
30. CD spinners
33. Beaver State

Puzzle 70

34. *Crimson Tide*, to fans

36. Range units: abbr.

37. Itty-bitty

39. Leaves out

40. West African nation

43. Italia's capital

44. Cut like a letter opener

45. Semester

46. "Paper or plastic?" item

47. Critical hosp. area

48. "…life is ___ a dream"

50. Enjoyment

Solution on Page 289

ACROSS

1. "Good buddy"
5. Parking area
8. Conceited people have big ones
12. ___ *Gun — Will Travel*
13. *Diamonds ___ Forever*
14. Part of USDA: abbr.
15. Utilizes
16. *Mystery!* network
17. ___-bitty
18. Trifling
19. Pulled the trigger
21. Sunbather's shade
24. Luxury watch brand
28. Tournament favorite
32. Tee shot
33. Gardner of Hollywood
34. Variety show
36. One in Bonn
37. Volcanic rock material
39. Famous vampire
41. Skirt fold
42. Under the weather
43. Parts of a min.
46. Sacha Baron Cohen character
50. Winter wear
53. Paving goo
55. Place to build
56. "___ delighted!" ("My pleasure!")
57. "Far out!"

58. Read cursorily
59. Fawn or doe
60. Dieters' units: abbr.
61. Strong urges

DOWN

1. Good buddy
2. Acid's opposite
3. "Be it ___ so humble…"
4. Turns back to zero
5. ___ of luxury
6. Spherical shapes
7. Former *Entertainment Tonight* co-host John
8. Masthead title
9. ___-up-and-go
10. Choose (to)
11. Hog's home
20. Tough time
22. Infuse with bubbles
23. Maiden name preceder
25. "In ___ of gifts…"
26. Good's opponent
27. Warrior princess of TV
28. Press down, as pipe tobacco
29. White House office shape
30. Senate errand runner
31. *Netflix* mailing
35. Psychic Geller
38. Top chess player

Puzzle 71

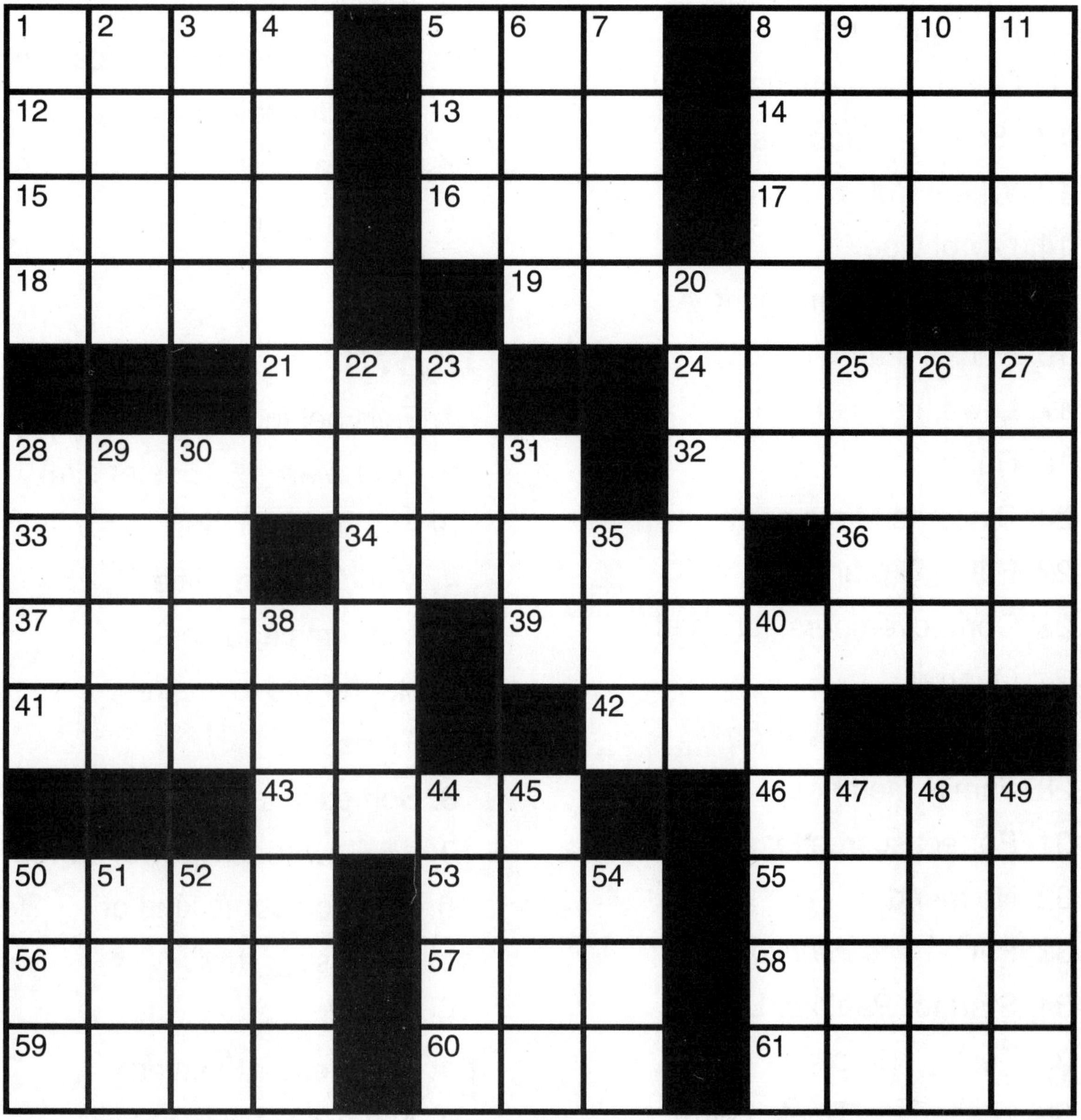

40. Elegantly stylish
44. Bottom-row PC key
45. Volvo rival
47. "I ___ Ike"
48. "Get ___ writing!"
49. Emeralds and diamonds
50. El ___ (Heston role)
51. "___ to a Nightingale"
52. Lincoln, informally
54. Hwys. and byways

Solution on Page 289

ACROSS

1. Columbo and others: abbr.
4. Honey makers
8. Credit union offering
12. "Say ___" (doctor's order)
13. Wheel rod
14. Cry of woe
15. Former telecom giant
16. Huck's craft
17. Lewd material
18. Rarely
20. Cinco de Mayo party
22. Put-___ (pranks)
23. Dorm overseers, for short
24. Quarrel
27. Deighton or Dawson
28. Family member
31. Perfect scores for divers
32. No friend
33. Pet on *The Flintstones*
34. Start for Paulo or Luis
35. Test-___ treaty
36. Lhasa ___ (Tibetan dog)
37. What to call an officer
38. Depot: abbr.
40. Truman who wrote *Breakfast at Tiffany's*
43. St. Francis of ___
47. Skillful server on the court
48. Claudia ___ Taylor (Lady Bird Johnson)
50. Dracula alter ego
51. Liver secretion
52. Whiskey drink
53. "I Like ___" ('50s political slogan)
54. Praiseful poems
55. Bikini parts
56. Rep.'s opponent

DOWN

1. Falls behind
2. *Little Man* ___ (Foster film)
3. Author Silverstein
4. Munchausen's title
5. Midterms and finals
6. North Pole toymaker
7. Release
8. Comes in last
9. ___ Law (basic law of current flow)
10. "Are you some kind of ___?"
11. "This is ___ toy"
19. Specks
21. 007 creator Fleming
24. Avenue crossers: abbr.
25. Potpie spheroid
26. Pitch ___-hitter
27. Chaney of horror films
28. Small drink
29. Write-___ (some votes)
30. Fan's rebuke
32. Orient
33. Rather and Rostenkowski

Puzzle 72

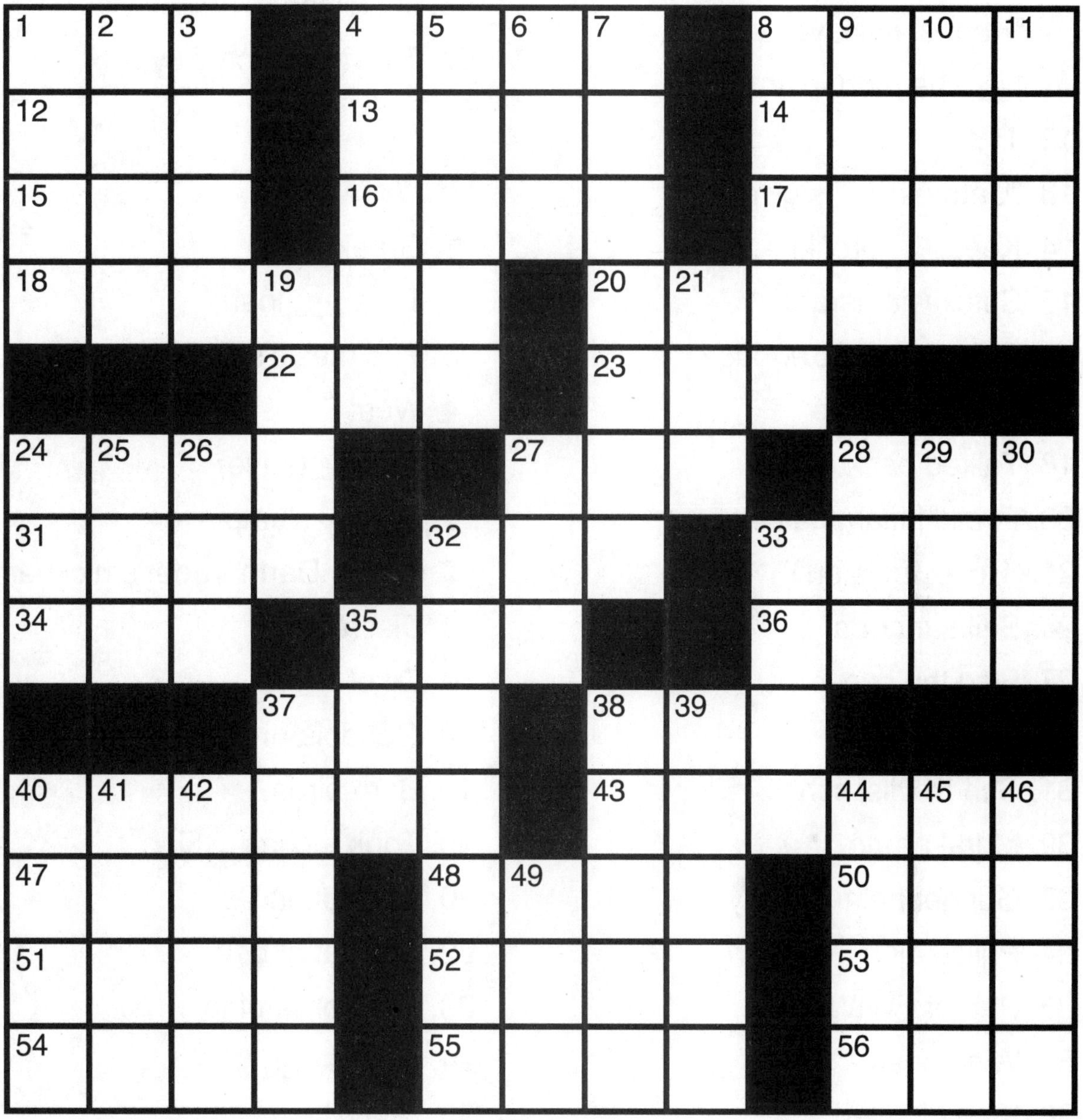

35. Took the bait
37. Painful spots
38. Stopped lying?
39. Romanov rulers
40. ___ San Lucas, Mexico
41. Corrosive liquid
42. Brazilian soccer legend
44. As before, in footnotes
45. Japanese drink
46. Thing on a list
49. English lavatory

Solution on Page 289

ACROSS

1. Machine tooth
4. "House" in Havana
8. "___ the mornin' to you!"
12. Tint
13. "Unto us ___ is given"
14. Keep ___ profile
15. Suffix with Israel
16. "Where ___ go wrong?"
17. Use the phone
18. Talked back to
20. Eyelid inflammations
21. "Relax, soldier!"
24. Sail supports
27. Fled the scene
28. Pull along
31. Sun Devils' sch.
32. Moral no-no
33. Guggenheim display
34. Police alert, for short
35. Part of FWIW
36. Wise ones
38. Kind of salad
40. In an unusual way
44. From square one
48. Eight on a sundial
49. Macpherson of *Sirens*
51. GI's mail drop
52. It's pumped in gyms
53. Plenty
54. B&O and Amtrak
55. Fender ding
56. Is obliged to
57. TV's "Science Guy"

DOWN

1. Greek X's
2. Take ___ loan
3. Pop music's Bee ___
4. West Point students
5. Set ___ (save)
6. Grassy clump
7. Young Darth Vader's nickname
8. Discretion
9. Oil of ___
10. Gondola propeller
11. Barn birds
19. Took a chair
20. 1 of 100 in DC
22. Get out of bed
23. ___ Bernardino
24. Goat's cry
25. Nile biter
26. Sizable sandwich
28. Children's game
29. Metal in rocks
30. Scale amts.
32. The bus stops here: abbr.
35. Wintry
36. Most secure

154

37. Train schedule abbr.
39. Smelling ___
40. Roman love poet
41. Potentially disastrous
42. Singer Celine
43. Dryer buildup
45. Bring in, as a salary

46. Energetic for one's age
47. Garden waterer
49. Sturdy tree
50. "Skip to My ___"

Solution on Page 290

ACROSS

1. Tobacco plug
5. Needle-bearing trees
9. Tanning lotion abbr.
12. Cry of pain
13. Diving bird
14. More than stretch the truth
15. Phi ___ Kappa
16. "Home on the Range" critter
18. K–O connection
20. Attention-getting shout
21. *The Zoo Story* playwright Edward
24. Gathers, as crops
28. Feed lines to
29. Goes out with
33. Abner adjective
34. Prefix with lateral
35. Generous ___ fault
36. "The Greatest" boxer
37. Use for an old T-shirt
38. Lightning and thunder event
40. He earns his pay at Shea
41. "Give it ___!"
43. At ___ for words
45. Poet's planet
47. Alternative to coffee
48. Guy known for his "Auld Lang Syne" rendition
52. End-of-week cry
56. "All ___ day's work"
57. Carpentry fastener
58. ___-Cola
59. Ghost's cry
60. Turned blonde, say
61. Broke new ground?

DOWN

1. Corn holder
2. Clamor
3. Perform on stage
4. Blubber source
5. Custard dessert
6. Tiny charged particle
7. Writer Philip
8. Nasty looks
9. Traffic caution
10. Dot on a die
11. Broker's charge
17. Strong alkaline
19. Kind of school
21. Integra maker
22. Moon-related
23. Light brown
25. Davy Crockett died defending it, with "the"
26. Stacks
27. Narrow cuts
30. Ma Bell
31. ___ many irons in the fire
32. "Wing" for Dumbo

156

38. Leave high and dry
39. West of the silver screen
42. Weep and wail
44. Door fastener
46. Jackass's sound
47. Informed
48. Ad-___ (improvise)

49. The woman of Lennon's "Woman"
50. Former Chinese chairman
51. Cube with 21 dots
53. Sticky stuff
54. Swelling reducer
55. It's all the rage

Solution on Page 290

ACROSS

1. King novel about a rabid dog
5. PC alternative
8. Roseanne, once
12. "The rest ___ to you"
13. "Turn to Stone" band
14. ___ tea
15. Father, to a baby
16. How some shall remain
18. Pete Seeger's genre
20. It's between Sun. and Tue.
21. Kind of wrestling
23. Perform better than
28. Dial-up alternative
31. Diaper problem
33. Submissive
34. Anticipates
36. Llama relative
38. Fiction's opposite
39. Green Hornet's sidekick
41. Memorial Day month
42. Youngsters
44. Front-page stuff
46. Out of the ordinary
48. "No ___ luck!"
51. Globetrotter's document
56. Bugs Bunny, e.g.
58. Transport, as a load
59. Cultural funding grp.
60. Auto loan default result
61. Frontiersman Crockett
62. Kenny G's instrument
63. Take ___ (go swimming)

DOWN

1. El ___ (Spanish hero)
2. Mil. fliers
3. Martial art
4. Iridescent gems
5. "All ___ are created equal"
6. Los ___, NM
7. "Round and Round" singer Perry
8. *The Family Circus* cartoonist Keane
9. ___ Ventura (Jim Carrey role)
10. Hi-___ image
11. Map lines: abbr.
17. Ambient music pioneer Brian
19. Actor Russell
22. Lone Ranger attire
24. Ballpark official
25. Sports group
26. Ten: prefix
27. Give the go-ahead
28. Foolish
29. Move to and fro
30. Be deficient in
32. Love's antithesis
35. Suffix with meteor
37. Temperature extremes
40. ___ *Doria* (ill-fated ship)
43. Apply bread to gravy

158

45. Kama ___

47. Puts on

49. For both sexes

50. Southwest Indian

51. Degree held by many univ.
professors

52. Motorists' org.

53. Ford Explorer, e.g.

54. Wily

55. IRS payment

57. M followers

Solution on Page 290

ACROSS

1. Hydroelectricity structure
4. Apr. 15 advisor
7. Obama predecessor
11. Wide shoe designation
12. "___ the ramparts we watched…"
13. Where Damascus is capital
14. Suffix with east or west
15. Singer Benatar
16. Camp shelters
17. Near the center of
18. Like Santa's cheeks
20. Mind-reading ability, for short
22. Singer Rawls
23. Youthful fellow
26. Covert ___ (CIA doings)
28. Rio Grande city
31. Knave
34. Pig sounds
35. Warnings
37. It may have 2 BRs
38. Banned insecticide
39. One of the Bobbsey twins
41. Six-pointers, for short
44. Argyle, e.g.
45. Sleep stage
47. Becomes corroded
51. Lamb's cry
53. Timetable abbr.
54. In progress
55. To do this is human
56. Pine-___
57. A.J. of racing
58. Possum's pouch
59. Weekend NBC hit, for short

DOWN

1. Regard as
2. Eagle's roost
3. Patches up
4. Speeder stopper
5. Bits of wisdom?
6. ___ Detoo
7. "Later!"
8. Large coffee maker
9. Take a chair
10. "Every dog ___ its day"
13. Pig's digs
19. Ambulance chaser's advice
21. Decant
23. Linked-computers acronym
24. "All you had to do was ___"
25. Uno + uno
27. Stroke gently
29. Slice (off)
30. Actor Brad
31. X-ray dose unit
32. Up there in years
33. "___ real!"
36. ___-Cone (summer snack)

37. Capital of Turkey

40. Highest points

42. Woman's apparel

43. ___ Hall (New Jersey university)

44. Fast jet, for short

46. Shopping mecca

47. UK military fliers

48. Flying saucer

49. Salty sauce

50. Wee one

52. Arrow's path

Solution on Page 290

ACROSS

1. Sign gases
6. Little bit
9. Scannable mdse. bars
12. Hang around for
13. Tip jar bill
14. Fam. reunion attendee
15. Taxi ticker
16. Took the blue ribbon
17. Code-breaking org.
18. Mongrel dogs
20. Fire-setting crime
22. Ponzi ___ (illegal investment)
25. Encouragement at the bullring
26. Tough row to ___
27. Courtyard
30. Hit the horn
32. Word before or after pack
33. Walk back and forth nervously
36. Calm
38. Chatter
39. Was ahead
40. In abundance
43. Frolics
46. "Play ___!"
47. Going through
48. ___ de Cologne
50. Become narrower
54. Shade tree
55. Satisfied sounds
56. Friend, south of the border
57. Reuben bread
58. "I tawt I taw a puddy ___"
59. Where the deer and the antelope play

DOWN

1. *Platoon* setting
2. Female in a flock
3. Mare's morsel
4. Nephew's sister
5. Play, as a ukulele
6. Pulls along behind
7. "I'll take that as ___"
8. National park in Alaska
9. Ash containers
10. Mexican currency
11. Extended family
19. Brought to maturity
21. Do another hitch
22. "Quiet, please!"
23. Dove's sound
24. Nest egg protectors?
25. Sandinista leader Daniel
28. Beach bum's shade
29. Cinco de ___
31. Kind of seaweed
34. Convertible or coupe, e.g.
35. ___ out (barely manage)
37. Return to office

41. Place to exchange rings

42. Andean animal

43. Winnebago owner, for short

44. Like service station rags

45. "Auntie" in a play

46. Head-and-shoulders sculpture

49. Solver's cry

51. ATM code

52. Omelet need

53. Fish-to-be

Solution on Page 291

ACROSS

1. Winter neckwear
6. Noah's boat
9. Carrier to Amsterdam
12. Number of little pigs or blind mice
13. Actress Thompson of *Back to the Future*
14. Mauna ___ (Hawaiian volcano)
15. Pub game
16. English ___ (coll. course)
17. Prefix with Asian
18. Drink from a flask
20. Gamblers place them
21. Navigational gizmo
24. "It follows that…"
26. Feel unwell
27. Bon Jovi's "___ of Roses"
28. Swift
32. Paper clip alternative
34. Bogart's hat
35. Check recipient
36. What cows chew
37. Escape, as from jail
38. "Oh, shucks!"
40. Mensa members have high ones
41. One of the five Ws
44. Fifty percent
46. Rightmost number on a grandfather clock
47. Hip-hop's ___ Def
48. Rice-___ ("The San Francisco Treat")
53. Kind of camera: abbr.
54. "It's no ___!"
55. Peace Nobelist Anwar
56. Layer
57. Everest and St. Helens
58. Exams

DOWN

1. Avg.
2. Chinese tea
3. Part of ETA
4. No longer working: abbr.
5. ___ up (come clean)
6. Joined by treaty
7. Have the throne
8. Krazy ___
9. Swiss artist Paul
10. Ill-mannered sort
11. Red planet
19. Cry on a roller coaster
20. Drop of sweat
21. Fight for breath
22. Bread with a pocket
23. Kill, as a dragon
25. Street ___ (reputation)
27. Huffed and puffed
29. ___ sci (college major, informally)
30. Baghdad's land
31. Beavers' creations

164

33. Bog material

34. Energy source for engines

36. Puts an end to

39. Apparition

41. Bit of smoke

42. San Francisco's Nob ___

43. Full of breezes

45. Like lightning

47. "___'s the word"

49. *Norma* ___ (Sally Field role)

50. Has too much

51. Turner who led a revolt

52. "___ a small world…"

Solution on Page 291

ACROSS

1. Talk show host Dr. ___
5. Letters after els
8. ___ pump (drainage aid)
12. Mongolian desert
13. Flower holder
14. Make bootees, e.g.
15. Part of a telephone number
17. Lotus-position discipline
18. Face off in the ring
19. ___ *Joey*
21. Running total
23. Breaks sharply
26. Gave medicine to
27. Protein-rich legume
29. What a quill may be dipped in
30. Actor Chaney
31. Bath site
32. Unnatural-sounding
35. Screen siren Garbo
37. ___ a time (individually)
38. Gaggle members
39. Prefix with center or cycle
40. Young ___ (kids)
41. Cornhusker St.
44. In direct confrontation
49. Chimney passage
50. School transport
51. Degree of speed
52. Swedish soprano Jenny
53. Hospital trauma ctrs.
54. Clock sound

DOWN

1. Links org.
2. Vert. opposite
3. "May ___ excused?"
4. Legally responsible
5. Powerful adhesive
6. *The ___ Squad* of '60s–'70s TV
7. Child by marriage
8. Bygone space station
9. Numero ___ (top dog)
10. Russian-built fighter aircraft
11. Sch. org.
16. Not hot
20. "Pick a number, ___ number"
21. Kemo Sabe's companion
22. Invite to enter
24. "For ___ sake!"
25. Fry lightly
26. Insult, in slang
27. Lawn makeup
28. Hoopsters' org.
30. 1970 Beatles chart-topper
33. Looked lecherously
34. Keg outlet
35. Mannerly man, briefly
36. Vacation spot
38. Surmise

41. Steelers' org.

42. Cotton gin inventor Whitney

43. Burger roll

45. "Give us this day ___ daily bread"

46. Mai ___ (bar order)

47. Where some stks. trade

48. Hair-raising cry

Solution on Page 291

ACROSS

1. Urban ride
4. Badminton barrier
7. Gas station machine
11. "Who ___ to say?"
12. Dude
13. WWII riveter
14. Prodigal ___
15. Not pro
16. Decorate
17. Harbor boat
18. Reps.' foes
20. Minister's title: abbr.
22. PC panic button
23. Poke
26. Breakfast drinks, briefly
28. African desert
31. Spirit in a bottle
34. Social standards
35. Butting heads
37. Driver's lic. and such
38. Alternatives to Macs
39. Spike TV, formerly
41. "___ the season…"
44. Twosomes
45. It doesn't detonate
47. Scold mildly
51. Snake that squeezes its prey
53. Word repeated after "If at first you don't succeed…"
54. WWII hero Murphy
55. Santa's helper
56. Get on in years
57. Sudden impulse
58. Rent out
59. Berlin's land: abbr.

DOWN

1. Players in a play
2. Stevie Wonder's "My Cherie ___"
3. Eat to excess
4. *SNL* network
5. Wears away
6. Musical sounds
7. Pea's home
8. Troop entertainment sponsor: abbr.
9. Former Russian space station
10. Animal enclosure
13. Dorm monitors: abbr.
19. Roast hosts, for short
21. Null and ___
23. Pickle container
24. The law has a long one
25. Some undergrad degs.
27. ___ Bartlet, president on *The West Wing*
29. "___ another thing…"
30. Party giver
31. Popular clothing store, with "The"
32. More of the same: abbr.
33. Items to crunch: abbr.

Puzzle 80

36. Sutcliffe of the early Beatles
37. Shoe cushion
40. ___ Peace Prize
42. Label with a name on it
43. Power glitch
44. Poor mark
46. Easter egg decorator
47. Raven's call
48. "What'd you say?"
49. Dictator Amin
50. Lower, as the lights
52. Toward the stern

Solution on Page 291

VACROSS

1. Shoo-___ (sure winners)
4. Dressed (in)
8. Eng. channel
11. Explorer Ericson
13. "Holy cow!"
14. Kuwaiti export
15. Vegas numbers game
16. Ride the waves
17. Certain boxing win, for short
18. Niagara Falls prov.
20. Expressed wonder
22. Fashion
25. Bake-off figure
27. London lav
28. Whole bunch
30. Roll up, as a sail
34. Mo. with no holidays
35. Fruit-filled pastries
37. Haw lead-in
38. Ship's prison
40. Put blacktop on
41. Three ___ kind
42. Historian's interest
44. Garden insect
46. "Blowin' in the Wind" composer
49. Patient-care grp.
50. Kanga's kid
51. Indiana birthplace of the Jackson 5
54. Female parents
58. Tiny Tim's instrument

59. Potato
60. Fourth-down play
61. Cut the grass
62. Toothpaste holder
63. Freight weight

DOWN

1. Sort
2. Jacqueline Bouvier Kennedy ___
3. ___ City (Las Vegas)
4. Abnormal sac
5. *Charlie's Angels* costar Lucy
6. Tax mo.
7. *Robinson Crusoe* author
8. The two of them
9. Kid's transport
10. Dirt clump
12. Put one over on
19. Egg-hatching spot
21. Not at work
22. Cut of marble
23. ___ de force
24. Bear or Berra
25. Diamond weight
26. Part of a home entertainment system
29. Bottle tops
31. "Here comes trouble!"
32. Mortgage adjustment, for short
33. Metal that Superman can't see through

170

36. Sewing line
39. Transcript fig.
43. Feeling of anxiety
45. "___ and Circumstance"
46. Bongo, for one
47. ___ Ono
48. MGM mogul Marcus

49. Jekyll's alter ego
52. Storekeeper on *The Simpsons*
53. Cause friction
55. ___ to lunch
56. L–P connection
57. RR stop

Solution on Page 292

ACROSS

1. Expensive fur
5. "___ do you do?"
8. Philanderer
11. More frosty
13. Carry-___ (some luggage)
14. Many moons ___
15. Suddenly run (at)
16. Kitten's plaint
17. Sack
18. Raised
20. Precursor of CDs
21. "Yecch!"
24. Alternative to .com or .edu
25. Letter after wye
26. Sailor
29. PC application file extension
31. Assumed name
32. High mark with low effort
36. Most common English word
38. Dozing
39. Felix or Garfield
41. A-Team muscleman
43. Seize
44. Go to seed
45. Magic sound effect
47. Dot-com's address
48. Sis or bro
49. As ___ (usually)
54. "Culpa" starter
55. Quid ___ quo
56. Evangelist ___ Semple McPherson
57. Lucky rabbit's foot, e.g.
58. "The best is ___ to come"
59. Gun sound

DOWN

1. Thickness measure
2. *ER* setting
3. Writer Anais
4. Frat party container
5. *The Simpsons* dad
6. Nervous as a cat
7. Opposite of ENE
8. Antenna alternative
9. Open-mouthed
10. Canines
12. Confederate soldier
19. *Apollo 13* director Howard
21. ___ *Today* (newspaper)
22. Hairdo stiffener
23. "Bali ___" (*South Pacific* song)
25. Enthusiasm
27. Damon of *Good Will Hunting*
28. Volcanic coating
30. Deletes, with "out"
33. Pol with a six-yr. term
34. Pro's vote
35. Alert to squad cars, briefly
37. *The ___ Strikes Back*

38. From ___ Z

39. Jazz pianist Chick

40. Attorney-___

42. Mechanical man

44. Roast cut

46. Air-safety agcy.

48. Snoop (on)

50. Lung protector

51. Thurman of *The Avengers*

52. Actor Cariou

53. Brain wave reading: abbr.

Solution on Page 292

ACROSS

1. Sound of disappointment
4. Scatters, as seed
8. Grand Ole ___
12. Tic-tac-toe victory
13. Conclude, with "up"
14. Earnest request
15. Yang's counterpart
16. Hair-raising
17. Kind of stick
18. Blackboard material
20. Major-___ (steward)
22. Week-___-glance calendar
24. Military denial
27. Directive as the judge enters
31. Storytelling uncle
33. Prickly seedcase
34. Canon competitor
36. Poem of tribute
37. Single-masted boat
39. Bauble
41. "___ we meet again"
43. Cell "messenger," briefly
44. Furniture wood
46. Hop out of bed
50. Mideast's ___ Strip
53. Microsoft Office component
55. Folk singer DiFranco
56. "___ Mommy Kissing Santa Claus"
57. Written reminder
58. Like a fiddle?
59. Nuts (over)
60. Distort, as data
61. Household sets

DOWN

1. Blocks, trains, tops, etc.
2. Potting material
3. Hawaiian coffee region
4. Term of endearment
5. Mine find
6. Fend (off)
7. Watch secretly
8. Be against
9. Mideast grp.
10. Std.
11. Hoopster ___ Ming
19. Paving material
21. Lawn moisture
23. Deadly cobra
25. Reply to "Are you hurt?"
26. Disrespectful
27. Muscles to crunch
28. Humdinger
29. Author Hubbard
30. Superlative suffix
32. Filming site
35. Hockey great Bobby
38. Canada's capital
40. Scot's refusal

174

42. Suburban expanses

45. Wacko

47. ___-Hartley Act

48. Inst. of higher learning

49. Peach centers

50. Musician's engagement

51. Cute ___ button

52. Zig's partner

54. Motorist's way: abbr.

Solution on Page 292

ACROSS

1. Capp and Gore
4. *48 Hours* network
7. Famed movie studio
10. ___ ex machina
12. Alley-___ (basketball maneuver)
13. Jeff Bridges' brother
14. Mitchell who sang "Big Yellow Taxi"
15. Go ___ rampage
16. Sitarist Shankar
17. Lemon peel
19. Passenger
20. Hot temper
23. Singer Feliciano
25. Yawn inducers
26. Wily
29. Govt. air-quality watchdog
30. Pro-___ (certain tourneys)
31. Not a happy camper
33. Fit for consumption
36. Reply to "Who's there?"
38. From soup to ___
39. Lesson from Aesop
40. Cake topping
43. Spoiled kid
45. Six-sided solid
46. Unknown John
47. Per unit
51. Brewski
52. Ltr. container
53. Lacking brightness
54. "No ___" (Chinese menu phrase)
55. QB's stats
56. *Alice* spin-off

DOWN

1. Modifying word: abbr.
2. DiCaprio, to fans
3. Natural tanner
4. Source of Davy Crockett's cap
5. 007's introduction
6. Hot tub
7. Lake formed by Hoover Dam
8. "I ___ at the office"
9. Sierra Club cofounder
11. "Yes ___, Bob!"
13. Lawyer's filing
18. April 15 org.
19. Q–U link
20. Civil War prez
21. Slangy denial
22. Cap and gown wearer
24. Sterile hosp. areas
27. Gorbachev was its last leader: abbr.
28. Tibet's Dalai ___
30. PC key near Ctrl
32. ___ Monte (food giant)
34. Kind of circle or tube

35. Annoy

36. "___ Loser" (Beatles song)

37. Lugged

40. Long-range weapon, for short

41. Pool sticks

42. "___ your pardon!"

44. Guns, as an engine

46. TV actress Susan

48. Alternative to "Woof!"

49. "Iron Man" Ripken

50. *Game of Thrones* channel

Solution on Page 292

ACROSS

1. Some USN officers
4. "Give ___ rest!"
7. "I should ___ lucky"
11. "...good witch ___ bad witch?"
12. No votes
14. Pitch-black
15. Substance in cigarettes
17. Monty Hall offering
18. God's honest truth
19. Suffix with Canton
21. Letters before ems
22. Chores
25. Peter the Great, for one
28. Wallflowerish
29. Mouthful of gum
31. ___ vu
32. U-turn from NNW
33. "All's ___ in love and war"
34. Amtrak stop: abbr.
35. Thesaurus wd.
36. Frees (of)
37. Wheel connectors
39. Faith Hill's "Take Me ___ Am"
41. Pumpkin-carving mo.
42. Garlicky shrimp dish
46. K–P connection
49. Greasy spoons
51. Suffix with techno-
52. "September ___" (Neil Diamond hit)
53. End-of-summer mo.
54. Uses a shovel
55. Auction unit
56. Cloud's locale

DOWN

1. Like a hippie's hair
2. Duo + one
3. Anatomical pouches
4. Computer chip maker
5. Coin-toss call
6. Rand who wrote *Atlas Shrugged*
7. ___ one's time (waits)
8. 180 degrees from WSW
9. Caribbean music
10. Olive ___
13. Bubble with rage
16. *The Magic Flute*, for one
20. "You don't ___!"
23. *The Bridge on the River ___*
24. The Shirelles' "Mama ___"
25. Savings acct. alternatives
26. Actress Catherine ___-Jones
27. "Stronger than dirt" sloganeer
28. Tax form ID
30. AMA members
32. Solar ___
33. Tuck, for one
35. Wall St. regulator
38. Pillages

39. The Jetsons' dog
40. What Fido follows
43. Young lady
44. Sneak a look
45. '60s TV show with Bill Cosby and
    Robert Culp
46. Digital readout, for short

47. Hosp. picture
48. Horse that's had it
50. "You've got mail" service

Solution on Page 293

ACROSS

1. TV monitoring gp.
4. Swiss mountain
7. Get ready, informally
11. "___ la la!"
12. Boxing match
14. Winter Olympics sled
15. King Kong, for example
16. Everglades beast
18. Clues, to a detective
20. Lowly chess piece
21. Golf ball's perch
22. Withstand
26. Distorts, as data
28. Put on a blacklist
29. Simon & Garfunkel, e.g.
30. ___ 500
31. They have Xings
32. ___ for oneself
33. Business VIP
34. "Don't ___ stranger"
35. Latin dance
36. Had a feeling
38. One skilled in CPR
39. *Star ___: The Original Series* (Shatner show)
41. Horse sound
44. Food fight site
48. Passing grade
49. Hoof sound
50. Apollo 11 destination
51. Green machine?
52. Autos
53. Slice
54. Place for a napkin

DOWN

1. Young horse
2. Get by somehow
3. Was unfaithful to
4. Degrades
5. Cyber guffaw
6. Solid parts of orange juice
7. Makes preparations
8. It's boring to be in one
9. A conceited person has a big one
10. Word before capita or annum
13. Queenly crowns
17. Singer Stefani
19. Moist, as morning grass
23. Like some twins
24. "Song ___ Blue" (Neil Diamond hit)
25. Heading for a chore list
26. Sets the dogs (on)
27. Midleg joint
28. Victoria's Secret product
31. Cash in, as coupons
32. Fortune's partner
34. Lahr or Parks
35. Renter

180

37. Staircase units

40. McDonald's founder Ray

42. "___ life!"

43. Rope fiber

44. New Deal agcy.

45. Fla. neighbor

46. In favor of

47. Lendee's note

Solution on Page 293

ACROSS

1. Pot's partner
4. Nonstick cooking spray
7. Makes docile
12. Dolt
13. One less than quadri-
14. Opera songs
15. "Love ___ neighbor…"
16. ___ Andreas fault
17. Defeats
18. Sweetie
19. Purchase offers
21. Office asst.
23. Timothy Leary's drug
24. Downing St. VIPs
27. Snacked on
29. Be pleasing (to)
32. Conductor Previn
35. Lion sounds
36. Piece of pasta
38. Took off
39. Ultimate degree
40. Bartender on *The Simpsons*
42. Empty spaces
46. Pelts
47. Medical research agcy.
48. "___ Jacques" (children's song)
52. Morse code word
54. ___ kwon do
55. Like ghost stories
56. Asner and Wynn
57. Suffix with hero
58. Complains
59. Member of the House, for short
60. Fold-up bed

DOWN

1. Hiking trails
2. "…old woman who lived in ___"
3. Justin Timberlake's former group
4. Quart divs.
5. Good for farming
6. Short skirts
7. Keep ___ on (watch)
8. "___ we having fun yet?"
9. Lead-in to hap or hear
10. End a fast
11. Serpent's warning
20. President before JFK
22. Three feet
24. Vegetable that rolls
25. Damage
26. Soon-to-be grads: abbr.
28. Part of AT&T: abbr.
30. Right to bear arms gp.
31. Ding's partner
32. Raggedy doll
33. *To Have and Have* ___
34. Play-___ (kids' clay)
37. Flightless Australian bird

38. Live (at)

41. "___ in the court!"

43. Shenanigan

44. Baby grand, e.g.

45. Piece of paper

46. Doctors' charges

48. Opposite of masc.

49. Antique auto

50. Mesozoic or Cenozoic

51. Tin Tin lead-in

53. Medicinal amt.

Solution on Page 293

ACROSS

1. "As I ___ saying…"
4. *Leaving ___ Vegas*
7. Moves quickly
11. Paintings, sculptures, etc.
12. "___ solemnly swear…"
13. Refrain in "Old MacDonald"
14. Noon, on a sundial
15. Juan or Carlos
16. Spread, as seed
17. Kyoto currency
18. "Head 'em off at the ___!"
20. Popular oil additive
22. La-la lead-in
23. Panhandle
26. Delivery room doctors, for short
28. BLT need
31. It may be acute or obtuse
34. Celebrity skewering
35. Cups, saucers, etc.
37. Internet pop-ups, e.g.
38. Captain's journal
39. One who looks Rover over
41. Tic-___-toe
44. "Stop right there!"
45. Cheer
47. Author of *The Divine Comedy*
51. "One," in Germany
53. TV maker
54. Roy's wife Dale
55. ___-Magnon man
56. Boater's blade
57. Shed some tears
58. Koppel or Kennedy
59. Stir-fryer

DOWN

1. Like paraffin
2. Sign before Taurus
3. Tour of duty
4. Jar top
5. Takes as one's own
6. Submarine detector
7. Teen blemish
8. Comparative suffix
9. Thanksgiving dessert
10. "You reap what you ___"
13. Feminine suffix
19. Warmed the bench
21. Campaign pros
23. Sheep's bleat
24. Non-earthlings, for short
25. *I've ___ a Secret*
27. The ___ Gees
29. Chicago airport code
30. Maximum
31. Home of the Braves: abbr.
32. Prefix with natal or classical
33. Comic's bit
36. New Deal proj.

184

37. Garb
40. Vote in
42. Cupid's projectile
43. Chocolate bean
44. "___ So Fine": 1963 #1 hit
46. "___! The Herald Angels Sing"
47. Drops on the grass

48. NYC's ___ of the Americas
49. Quick snooze
50. Demolition stuff
52. Signal approval

Solution on Page 293

ACROSS

1. Mayhem
6. Cloak and dagger org.
9. Bandleader Severinsen
12. Protein-building acid
13. Ques. counterpart
14. A Gabor sister
15. Place for a squirting flower
16. Picnic scurrier
17. Moon-roving vehicle
18. Pulled apart
20. Jockey's handful
22. Pay no mind to
25. Watergate prosecutor Archibald
26. SSW's opposite
27. Humiliated
30. Gave a signal to
32. "Dear ___ or Madam"
33. Sea creature that moves sideways
36. Take down a notch
38. Santa ___ winds
39. Ages and ages
40. On cloud nine
43. Almanac tidbits
46. QB Tarkenton
47. Savings option, briefly
48. Suffix with Gator
50. Deprive of weapons
54. 100 cts.
55. Wrath
56. CB, for one
57. Have debts
58. Cartoon collectible
59. Throw for ___ (surprise)

DOWN

1. Holbrook or Linden
2. Drs.' group
3. Big shot, briefly
4. ___ a customer
5. Use crayons
6. James of TV's *Las Vegas*
7. Quaint lodging
8. Houston team
9. Sub shop
10. Baking chamber
11. Rotating engine parts
19. Use one's noodle
21. Corporate bigwig, for short
22. *Monsters, ___* (2001 Pixar film)
23. Bearded grassland dweller
24. "___ I say more?"
25. Life's work
28. Small part
29. "Phooey!"
31. Mosquito repellent ingredient
34. Suffix with meth- or eth-
35. Like Leroy Brown
37. Artwork made of tiles
41. Mrs. Bush

186

42. One year's record
43. Generic pooch
44. In ___ (lined up)
45. NASCAR's Yarborough
46. Touch
49. Rap's Dr. ___
51. Bother

52. Wayne film ___ *Bravo*
53. Floor-washing aid

Solution on Page 294

ACROSS

1. Supplement
6. Hole puncher
9. ___ room (play area)
12. Long (for)
13. Restaurant bill
14. Paul Bunyan's tool
15. Break off a relationship
16. Is it Miss or ___?
17. Sn, chemically speaking
18. Explorer Marco
20. Sudden shock
21. Oinker
24. Daddies
25. Bowling alley divisions
26. Layered sandwich, briefly
27. Longtime senator Thurmond
29. Heavy hammer
32. Classify
36. Slipup
38. Cry of disgust
39. ___ of Two Cities
42. Sheriff's asst.
44. Duet number
45. ___ weevil
46. Wind resistance
48. Losing tic-tac-toe row
49. Garbage bag securer
51. Indy competitor
55. Great noise
56. Uncertainties
57. Mall booth
58. Where London is: abbr.
59. Cambridge univ.
60. ___-Saxon

DOWN

1. Sailor's "yes"
2. Room with an easy chair
3. Father figure
4. Journey
5. "___ of Old Smokey"
6. Maximally
7. ___ of 1812
8. Scale amts.
9. Boca ___, FL
10. Napoleon's fate
11. Pennies
19. Modern surgical tool
20. Photocopier problems
21. *Frontline* airer
22. Feeling poorly
23. Verizon forerunner
25. ___ Altos, Calif.
28. More unusual
30. Big name in computers
31. Test for college srs.
33. Choose
34. Like steak tartare
35. However, briefly

37. Most bizarre

39. Dwelling

40. Poisonous substance

41. Parallel to

43. Hooded jacket

47. Loss's opposite

49. Director Burton

50. ___ *Were King*

52. Gear part

53. Immigrant's course: abbr.

54. *King Kong* studio

Solution on Page 294

ACROSS

1. Alternatives to PCs
5. Day-___ colors
8. "Hey you!"
11. Alka-Seltzer sound
12. Once around the sun
14. GI's address
15. Prefix with pad or port
16. Leaf gatherer
17. Regret
18. French ___ soup
20. Wicked one
22. Gumbo vegetables
24. Like a matador's cape
25. King's domain
26. Freeway entrance
29. Not Rep. or Dem.
30. Blvds.
31. White House spokesman Fleischer
33. Coin flips
36. "No problem!"
38. ___-inspiring
39. Unifying idea
40. In one piece
43. Church singing group
45. "That hits the spot!"
46. Unmixed
48. ___ to riches
51. Perimeter
52. ___ on (trampled)
53. Like bachelor parties
54. Use a lever
55. "If looks could kill" type of stare
56. Pinball infraction

DOWN

1. Dashboard abbr.
2. Drink on draught
3. Grand Canyon river
4. Of the backbone
5. Greek sandwich
6. Low-fat, as beef
7. Country music's ___ Ridge Boys
8. Remove, as a potato peel
9. Made a web
10. ___ the line (obeyed)
13. Allude (to)
19. Belief suffix
21. Neighbor of Wyo.
22. "It must be him, ___ shall die…" (Vikki Carr line)
23. Clark of the *Daily Planet*
24. Hosp. workers
26. NFL tiebreakers
27. Grand Prix racer
28. High school dance
30. "Get it?"
32. Jack's preceder
34. "My gal" of song
35. Cleaned the floor

190

36. "What am ___ do?"

37. Need for water

40. Distort

41. Head covering

42. "Goodness!"

43. Relative of a gator

44. Actress Lamarr

47. Debunked mentalist Geller

49. Guy's honey

50. ___ Pepper

Solution on Page 294

ACROSS

1. Sleepwear, briefly
4. Withdrew, with "out"
9. Chime in
12. It's perpendicular to long.
13. Prop up
14. Attorney F. ___ Bailey
15. End of a student's email address
16. Fable writer
17. Memorable films cable sta.
18. Overalls material
20. "To thine ___ self…"
22. Pas' partners
24. Pilfers
27. "I say, old ___"
30. Facial spasm
32. Tortoiselike
33. Writer Fleming
34. Gardner of *On the Beach*
35. ER pronouncement
36. Boxing venue
38. Stimpy's sidekick
39. Soccer great Mia
40. Skeleton's place?
42. Mao ___-tung
44. "You're it!" game
45. Furious
49. ___ Na Na
51. Be a cast member of
55. Stephen of *Michael Collins*
56. Where a rabbit may be hidden
57. Extinguish
58. Every little bit
59. Iris's place
60. Dirty campaign tactic
61. "Science Guy" Bill

DOWN

1. Answered a charge in court
2. Green gemstone
3. Sci-fi phaser setting
4. Bush successor
5. "Med" or "law" lead-in
6. Some univ. instructors
7. Environmentalist's prefix
8. Train stop
9. "Hawkeye" Pierce portrayer
10. Not Rep. or Ind.
11. Christmas mo.
19. Little devil
21. Film director Craven
23. Get the ball rolling
24. Hardly enough
25. Appear ominously
26. Did laps in a pool
27. Newspaper sales fig.
28. Signal, as a cab
29. Comment on, as in a margin
31. "___ seen worse"
37. Govt. property overseer

Puzzle 92

39. Cooped clucker
41. Antiquated exclamation
43. More rational
46. Gramp's wife
47. Trust, with "on"
48. George Bush's alma mater
49. "___ Drives Me Crazy" (Fine Young Cannibals hit)
50. Farm bale
52. Common URL ender
53. Election Day, e.g.: abbr.
54. *Happiness ___ Warm Puppy*

Solution on Page 294

ACROSS

1. Locate
5. Horned animal
8. Scissorhands portrayer Johnny
12. Mayberry lad
13. Contend (for)
14. Jai ___
15. Klutz's utterance
16. ___ League
17. Hatchling's home
18. Wight, for one
20. Songs for two
21. Explosive liquid, for short
24. Blunder
26. Partner of pains
27. Warms up again
31. ___ tai (cocktail)
32. Bad spell
33. Pen name
34. Catch in a trap
37. Steam bath
39. "___ Lonesome I Could Cry"
40. Step inside
41. Back street
44. Actress Meg
46. Bric-a-___
47. Pharmaceuticals watchdog agcy.
48. Rock band boosters
52. Prospector's bonanza
53. It may be glossed over
54. Han Solo's love
55. Finishes
56. Green light
57. Open-handed blow

DOWN

1. Egg ___ yung
2. Stock mkt. debut
3. Bite like a pup
4. Name of Tennessee's streetcar
5. The dark force
6. Motto of New Hampshire
7. Door opener
8. River in a Strauss waltz
9. Gen. Robert ___
10. It might be checkered
11. Racetrack stops
19. Message from the *Titanic*
20. "Obviously!"
21. "Hello!" sticker info
22. "___ See Clearly Now"
23. That's partner
25. ___ Luthor of *Superman*
28. Neighbor on
29. Fork prong
30. Surgery souvenir
32. 60-min. units
35. Sisters' daughters
36. TV's *Judging* ___
37. Poseidon's domain

194

38. Yearly records
41. ___-bodied seaman
42. Scientologist Hubbard
43. Alan or Cheryl
45. Kennel cries
47. Fishing lure
49. Singer Tormé

50. Entertainer Zadora
51. Maple syrup source

Solution on Page 295

ACROSS

1. FM station employees
4. Kindergarten basics
8. Doorway welcomer
11. Hammer's target
13. Angry outburst
14. Sounds of hesitation
15. Wing ___ prayer
16. ___ cost (free)
17. Restaurant bill addition
18. Boy king of Egypt
20. Country singer Buck
22. "___ your instructions…"
25. White House assistant
27. Windy City, for short
28. Pre-coll. exams
30. Actress Spelling
34. "On ___ of Old Smokey"
35. Buenos ___, Argentina
37. Classroom replacement
38. Beef and vegetables dish
40. Get together
41. Skirt's edge
42. Lighten, as a burden
44. Accumulate, as a fortune
46. Competed in the Indy 500
49. Dubya's deg.
50. Somewhat: Suffix
51. Palindromic pop quartet
54. Sounds from pounds
58. Sporty Pontiac
59. Lunch or dinner
60. Stubborn beast
61. Just enough to wet the lips
62. Eyelid problem
63. Yup's opposite

DOWN

1. Genetic ID
2. Dean's singing partner
3. Comic Caesar
4. Smell ___ (be suspicious)
5. Belfry denizen
6. MSNBC rival
7. Got to one's feet
8. Remote control button
9. Infamous Idi
10. Recipe measures: abbr.
12. Running behind
19. ___ Major (Big Dipper's constellation)
21. Dripping
22. Divisions of a play
23. Gun blast
24. Sherlock Holmes item
25. Up ___ (cornered)
26. Fortune-teller's phrase
29. Points (at)
31. Construction site watchdog, for short
32. Regrets
33. Some early PCs

196

36. Attack with a knife
39. Pint-sized
43. John or John Quincy
45. Sir's counterpart
46. Big trucks
47. ___ spumante wine
48. Sharp blow in karate

49. Masculine
52. Take the odds
53. San Francisco/Oakland separator
55. Seek office
56. Ala. neighbor
57. Use a needle

Solution on Page 295

ACROSS

1. Meat in a can
5. Summit
9. Delta rival
12. Well-___ (rich)
13. Stir up
14. Talk, talk, talk
15. Tavern mugfuls
16. Pole, e.g.
17. "The ___ and the Pendulum"
18. Hershey competitor
20. Doctrines
22. Nervousness
24. Educ. institution
27. Old Dodger great Hodges
28. Use an eggbeater
32. Each, informally
34. Wrigley Field player
36. Filly's father
37. Coffeehouse crockery
38. ___ *Rheingold*
40. Slide down a slope
41. UFO crew
44. Subsides
47. Bjorn Borg's homeland
52. Stewart who sang "Maggie May"
53. Engrave with acid
55. "Keep it coming!"
56. Commando weapon
57. Inlet
58. Being nothing more than
59. Persona ___ grata
60. Fire hydrant attachment
61. Entry-level position: abbr.

DOWN

1. Ollie's partner in old comedy
2. Barbershop emblem
3. Lemon and orange drinks
4. A majority
5. Poison in classic mysteries
6. Rank below general: abbr.
7. Sporty Mazda
8. Santa's helpers
9. Hunt and peck
10. "Just a sec!"
11. Rental units: abbr.
19. ___ nut (wheel fastener)
21. Part of CNN
23. Escape capture by
24. Walton who founded Walmart
25. Intel product, briefly
26. Greedy type
29. ___ Master's Voice
30. Drive up the wall
31. I.M. the architect
33. HS junior's test
35. Wailer of Irish folklore
39. Opposite of NNE
42. Bloodsucker

Puzzle 95

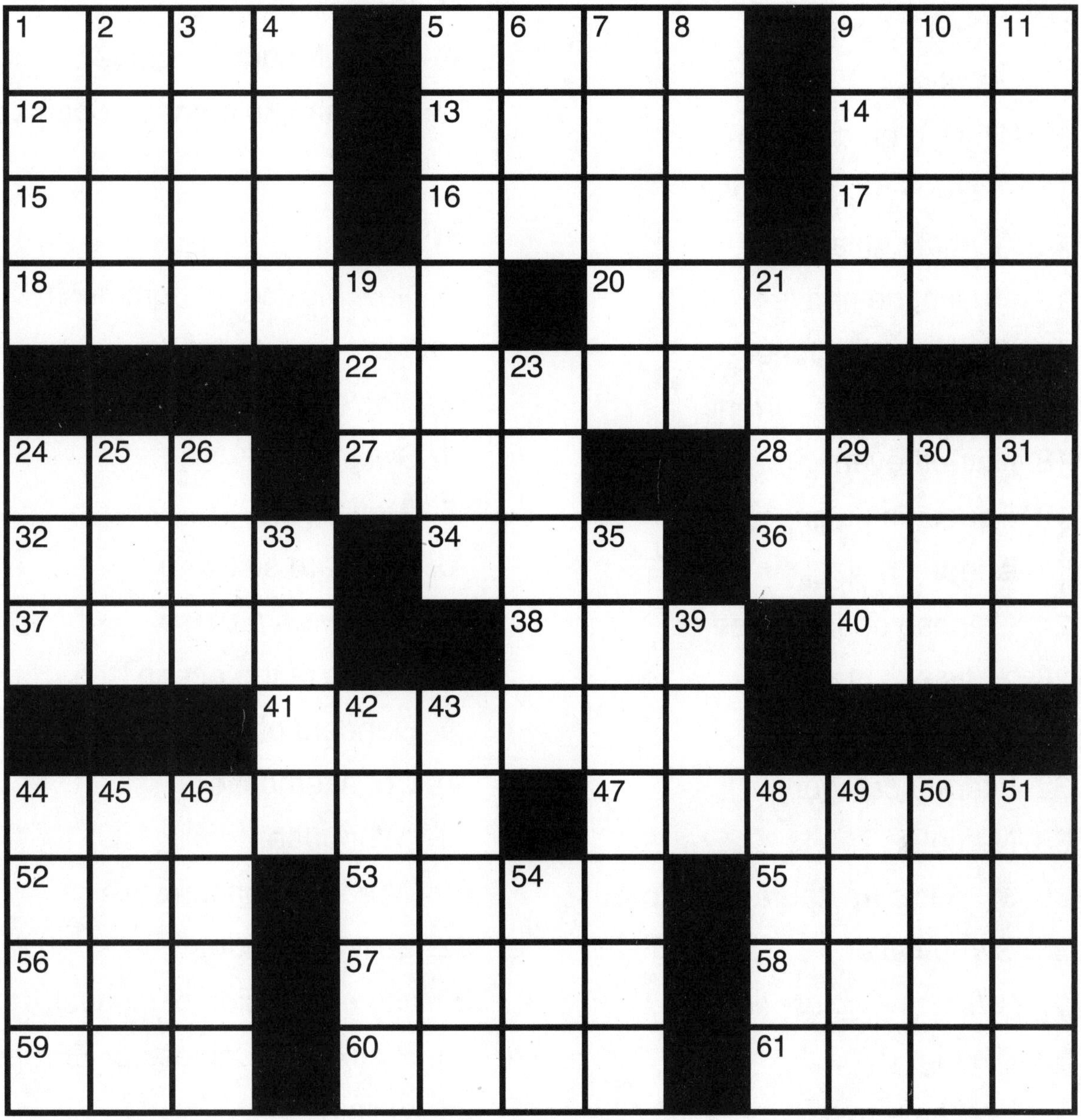
1
2
3
4
5
6
7
8
9
10
11
12
13
14
15
16
17
18
19
20
21
22
23
24
25
26
27
28
29
30
31
32
33
34
35
36
37
38
39
40
41
42
43
44
45
46
47
48
49
50
51
52
53
54
55
56
57
58
59
60
61

43. "Life ___ short…"
44. Give ___ for one's money
45. ___ the clown
46. Tennis score
48. Thompson of *Sense and Sensibility*
49. Deer moms
50. Fumbles
51. Hair No More alternative
54. Rite Aid competitor

Solution on Page 295

ACROSS

1. Bugler's evening call
5. What Horton heard
8. Merely
12. "Hurry!" on a memo
13. *Playboy* mogul, to pals
14. Animal rights org.
15. Muskogee native
16. Thanksgiving tuber
17. Circular water current
18. Half-off event
19. Equestrian's grip
21. Adept
24. Chinese or Japanese
28. "...fish ___ fowl"
31. Certain sib
32. Literary category
33. Narcotic
35. ___ Vic's (restaurant chain)
36. Syrup flavor
37. "With all ___ respect..."
38. Big lug
39. Borden's cow
40. Former mates
42. ___ *for All Seasons*
44. Playbill listing
48. Deuces
51. Hanks film
53. ___ breve (2/2 time)
54. Radiate, as charm
55. Weep
56. Jet engine sound
57. Peat source
58. Joe DiMaggio's brother
59. Big name in computer games

DOWN

1. New Mexico art community
2. "May I ___ favor?"
3. Mop's companion
4. Swiftness
5. "How come?"
6. Red card suit
7. "You want a piece ___?"
8. Middle of the ocean
9. Flanders of *The Simpsons*
10. Co. alternative
11. "Whoopee!"
20. Words of concurrence
22. Self-___ (pride)
23. Old expression of disgust
25. Prefix with Chinese or European
26. Vicinity
27. Squishy ball brand
28. Alaskan city near the Arctic Circle
29. October's birthstone
30. Steals, with "off"
34. Assumed names
35. Prom rental
37. Robert of *Goodfellas*

41. Marks for life
43. Start of an alphabet song
45. Soothing agent
46. Smelting waste
47. Scarlett's home
48. ___ Sawyer
49. Wine and dine, say

50. Wt. units
52. Workout facility

Solution on Page 295

ACROSS

1. "Phew!" inducer
5. They give people big heads
9. Average guy
12. ___ erectus
13. TV's Nick at ___
14. Oscar-winning director Lee
15. Christmas greenery
17. Eggy drink
18. Atmosphere
19. Selects from the menu
21. Disheveled
24. Luau garland
25. Queen of mystery
26. Double-___ sword
29. Winter woe
30. *The Karate* ___ (1984)
32. Shorthand pro, for short
36. Greek goddess of wisdom
39. Panel truck
40. Sprinkle with spices
41. Dwell (on)
44. Golf goal
45. Lard, essentially
46. Photographer's case
51. Cook in oil
52. Comedian King
53. Sushi bar drink
54. Topic for Dr. Ruth
55. There are 435 in Cong.
56. Fraud

DOWN

1. Electrical resistance unit
2. ___ *Hear a Waltz?*
3. Meditative sounds
4. Spin on an axis
5. The E in Einstein's formula
6. "Vamoose!"
7. Peter of *My Favorite Year*
8. Become enraged
9. Author Austen
10. ___ about (approximately)
11. Omelet ingredients
16. Tall tale teller
20. Understand, in hippie lingo
21. Yellow card issuer
22. ___ *Well That Ends Well*
23. Excess supply
27. Barely gets by, with "out"
28. Flintstones' pet
31. Quarterback Marino
33. December 24, e.g.
34. Winston Cup org.
35. Bargain-hunter's favorite words
36. Colorado trees
37. Eye drop
38. Bother continually
41. Wastes, in mob slang
42. Unadorned

43. River of the underworld

47. Cartographer's concern

48. "___, humbug!"

49. Alias, for short

50. The ___ State (Idaho)

Solution on Page 296

ACROSS

1. Junkyard dog's greeting
4. Ginger cookie
8. That guy
11. Theater award
13. Bit of verbal fanfare
14. Are ___ for real?
15. "What ___ do to deserve this?"
16. Looker
17. Extinguish, with "out"
18. Stanley Cup gp.
20. Catholic clergyman
22. Sex ___
25. From A ___
26. Remote control abbr.
27. Crib cry
29. Big books
33. "Now ___ me down to sleep"
35. Bacardi product
37. Painter of melting watches
38. Actress Braga
40. "That's show ___!"
42. Jury-___ (improvise)
43. Place to play darts
45. Straighten up
47. Stick (to)
50. Tooth pro's deg.
51. Seoul-based automaker
52. Klutzes
54. Uncertain
58. ICU drips
59. Cartoonist Goldberg
60. None too happy
61. "No thanks"
62. Keep ___ (persist)
63. Republicans, for short

DOWN

1. The Almighty
2. Baseball stat
3. Cleansed (of)
4. Outstanding
5. Yea's opposite
6. Very skilled
7. Repeat
8. Hoopla
9. Bettors' promises, e.g.
10. Mixed-breed dog
12. "___ kleine Nachtmusik"
19. "Hee ___"
21. Polo shirt brand
22. Budget competitor
23. Prince Charles's sport
24. Prepare for the future
28. Wheel's center
30. Wal___
31. Writer Wiesel
32. Communicate by hand
34. "Egad!"
36. Way of thinking

204

39. ___ borealis (northern lights)

41. A's opposite, in England

44. Doozy

46. Without any guarantees

47. Very similar

48. Prima donna

49. Food that's "slung"

53. "Ten Most Wanted" agcy.

55. London forecast

56. To's reverse

57. "You betcha!"

Solution on Page 296

ACROSS

1. Capote, for short
4. Rumple, as hair
8. ___ as it is
12. Soap unit
13. "Be ___!" ("Help me out!")
14. Sounds of laughter
15. Letters on a Cardinal's cap
16. Missile housing
17. Impressed
18. Mexican moolah
20. End-of-the-week cry
22. Leap day's mo.
24. Male deer
28. Worry (about)
31. Actress Jessica
34. Enemy
35. Financial support
36. Double reeds
37. Column crosser
38. "Man's best friend"
39. Goldie of *Laugh-In* fame
40. Mama's boys
41. Beer holder
43. When repeated, a Gabor
45. Betsy or Diana
48. Layers of paint
52. "Look ___ (I'm in Love)"
55. Prefix with -naut
57. "___ voyage!"
58. "___ only trying to help"
59. ___ as a pin
60. Heat meas.
61. Coin factory
62. Depletes, as strength
63. Stick up

DOWN

1. Recipe abbr.
2. Interest figure
3. Web addresses, for short
4. En ___ (as a group)
5. AP rival
6. Sodium chloride
7. Trudge
8. Mine passage
9. Big Detroit inits.
10. Guerrilla Guevara
11. "I've ___ it up to here!"
19. Frequently, in poems
21. "Your guess ___ good…"
23. "Ali ___ and the Forty Thieves"
25. Jimi Hendrix hairdo
26. Hired thug
27. Uses needle and thread
28. Short-lived crazes
29. Urban unrest
30. Sharp side of a knife
32. Nearing depletion
33. Mercedes-___

36. "This can't be!"

40. ___ Tome and Principe

42. "___ my case"

44. Glasgow residents

46. ___ serif (font choice)

47. "___ penny, pick it up…"

49. Etc., for one

50. In ___ (completely)

51. Rebuff

52. Look through the crosshairs

53. Prefix with night or light

54. "___ overboard!"

56. Puff Daddy's genre

Solution on Page 296

ACROSS

1. Decade divs.
4. iPhone download
7. Kaput sound
11. ___ the line (obey)
12. Take off, as weight
14. Suffix with million
15. Cover the gray
16. Aloha gifts
17. Cereal "for kids"
18. Pornography
20. %: abbr.
22. Nicholas I or II
23. Kudos
26. Newscaster Couric
27. ___ Van Winkle
28. *The ___ of Pooh*
30. "It's ___ world": Dickens
31. Bon ___ (witty saying)
32. Insurer's exposure
33. *Morning Edition* network
34. Hippie's home
35. Fishing rods
36. Chinese, e.g.
38. "___ never fly!"
39. Poli ___
40. Baseball's Hershiser
41. Bilko and Pepper: abbr.
44. Cadabra preceder
46. Billy Joel's "___ to Extremes"
49. "Mon ___!"
50. What you pay
51. Not a lot
52. "She Believes ___" (Kenny Rogers song)
53. Tale of ___
54. Slippery one

DOWN

1. Since 1/1: abbr.
2. Cowboy Rogers
3. Experiences dizziness
4. Magnetism
5. Walt Whitman, for one
6. Letters on a tire
7. Singer Page
8. Spruce relative
9. TGIF day
10. Country singer Ritter
13. ___ de corps
19. Housekeeper
21. Salary ceiling
22. Home of the NFL's Buccaneers
23. Nudges
24. Fruit bowl painting
25. Painter's stand
26. Topeka is its cap.
29. Approves
31. Lunatic
32. Learning method

208

34. Lobbying org.

35. Jolly Roger flier

37. Number of a magazine

40. Roughly

41. "Star Wars" program, for short

42. ___ rummy

43. Pro ___ (for now)

45. Gift adornment

47. "Golly!"

48. Bird that gives a hoot

Solution on Page 296

ACROSS

1. L.A. campus
4. Dead-___ street
7. Elephant of children's lit
12. Mom's mate
13. Peace sign shape
14. Apprehensive
15. Dire ___, rock group
17. Quarrel
18. Prescription writers: abbr.
19. Fine sprays
20. Circle or square
23. Govt. narcotics watchdog
24. Vim and vigor
25. Sports org. with a March tourney
28. Property damage, to an insurer
32. AOL or EarthLink, for example: abbr.
33. Dining room furniture
35. Agcy. for homeowners
36. Singer Cole et al.
38. Bakery worker
39. Hunky-dory
40. All you ___ eat
42. Queen ___ lace
44. Without ___ in the world
47. CBS police series
48. Thesaurus compiler
49. Golf reservation
53. Pacific or Atlantic
54. Woody Allen's *Hannah and ___ Sisters*
55. Reggae's Marley
56. ___ *Rae*
57. Battleship letters
58. Rioting crowd

DOWN

1. Downs' partner
2. Tippler
3. EMT's forte
4. Obvious
5. Butterfly snarers
6. ___ Plaines, Illinois
7. Hold responsible
8. Antenna
9. Panhandles
10. In ___ (going nowhere)
11. Dark loaves
16. Fuse rating unit
20. *Wheel of Fortune* action
21. "For ___ jolly good fellow"
22. Date with a Dr.
23. Racing legend Earnhardt
26. Brother of Abel
27. Alphabetical network
29. The end ___ era
30. Oxford or loafer
31. Fifth Avenue landmark
34. Pencil ends

37. Sound of fright

41. MetLife competitor

43. Louse-to-be

44. Elvis Presley's middle name

45. Couturiere Chanel

46. Finish for teen or golden

47. So-so marks

49. Wed. follower

50. ThinkPad developer

51. Bovine utterance

52. Flow back

Solution on Page 297

ACROSS

1. "Mind your ___ business!"
4. "How can ___ sure?"
7. In favor of
10. Pod contents
12. Number of pool pockets
13. Dud
14. Divide
16. Cheerful tune
17. Nov. 11 honoree
18. Film vault collection
19. ___ pole
22. One of Hamlet's options
24. Small bills
25. Like a phoenix out of the ashes
28. Show hosts, for short
29. Runs in neutral
31. Brazilian vacation spot, informally
33. Cultural, as cuisine
35. Shopping center
36. Cash dispensers, for short
37. Checked out, as before a heist
38. Motionless
41. Engine sound
42. ___ avail (hopeless)
43. False appearance
48. Tabloid fliers
49. '50s prez
50. *Bill & ___ Excellent Adventure*
51. Habit wearer
52. Silent acknowledgment
53. Disposable pen maker

DOWN

1. Special ___ (military force)
2. Minuscule
3. Afternoon snooze
4. "Peace ___ hand"
5. Drill attachment
6. Palindromic English river
7. Ballet movement
8. Rock's partner
9. Makes a choice
11. Rescues
13. Skedaddles
15. Sleep acronym
18. Score-producing stats
19. Actor Selleck
20. "___ upon a time…"
21. Midterm or final
22. Bathroom powders
23. Metal-in-the-rough
26. Historic periods
27. Christie's *Death on the ___*
29. Part of IHOP: abbr.
30. Poorly lit
32. Like octogenarians
34. Angels' headgear
35. *Glengarry Glen Ross* playwright David

37. Director's cry
38. Zap with a Taser
39. Soybean product
40. Barge ___ (interrupt)
41. Take seriously
43. Wrestling win
44. *It's a Wonderful Life* studio

45. Kan. neighbor
46. Reagan-era mil. program
47. Computer key

Solution on Page 297

ACROSS

1. Post's opposite
4. Utah ski spot
8. So it would ___ (apparently)
12. Co. that merged with Time Warner
13. Crotchety oldster
14. Alan of *Manhattan Murder Mystery*
15. Strong cleaner
16. Money drawer
17. Move like a moth
18. Bullwinkle, for one
20. Track contests
21. Spotless
23. "___ I say, not…"
25. Dryer residue
26. West German capital
27. Doctrine: Suffix
30. Respiratory disorder
32. Deficiency of red blood cells
34. TDs are worth six
35. Muffin material
37. Untamed
38. Check someone's ID
39. Starbucks selection
40. Windows predecessor
43. Ex-Mrs. Trump
45. Word of woe
46. "Cool, man!"
47. Egypt's King ___
50. Falling-out
51. Detective's assignment
52. Rock producer Brian
53. CPR experts
54. Not an abstainer
55. Tofu source

DOWN

1. Buddy
2. Singer Orbison
3. Strunk and White's *The ___ of Style*
4. Take steps
5. Lane of the *Daily Planet*
6. "Holy" Ohio town
7. Capital of Ga.
8. Vaults
9. Model Macpherson
10. Spruce up a manuscript
11. Cushions for tumblers
19. Swearing-in words
20. *Death in Venice* author
21. Show appreciation at a performance
22. Grocery shopper's aid
24. ___ empty stomach
26. *Roseanne* star
27. Acts like
28. Delta deposit
29. Fashioned

Puzzle 103

31. Wharton degs.

33. McGregor of Star Wars films

36. New Balance competitor

38. Expenses

39. Brewery product

40. Stallion's mate

41. Slight, as chances

42. Off one's rocker

44. Carpenter's clamp

46. Post-op locale

48. Numero ___

49. Thing to play with

Solution on Page 297

ACROSS

1. Head out to sea
5. Quick swims
9. ___ Paulo
12. Swindles
13. Good-sized plot
14. Author Rand
15. The "I" of *The King and I*
16. Cat's plaint
17. "I never ___ a man I didn't like"
18. Hatchlings' homes
20. Homes
22. Oregon city
24. Golf peg
27. Companion of Tarzan
28. Soprano Gluck
32. Coral rings
34. Jerusalem's land
36. Grandmother, affectionately
37. Magnate Onassis
38. "That ___ close"
39. Diminish
42. Newton and Stern
44. Long stories
49. Penn in NYC, e.g.
50. "Bubble, bubble, ___ and trouble…"
52. Sonny of Sonny and Cher
53. Negative replies
54. As a result
55. "___ girl!"
56. Fireworks reaction
57. City near Tahoe
58. Job to do

DOWN

1. Read a bar code
2. Tip-top
3. B&Bs
4. Aspiring atty.'s exam
5. Beaver's project
6. Frigid epoch
7. Investigate
8. Attach with needle and thread
9. "___ to you, buddy!"
10. Affirmative votes
11. Toronto's loc.
19. Close, as an envelope
21. "___ Diary…"
23. Downs' opposite
24. Light brown
25. Inbound flight approx.
26. Years and years
29. Attorney's profession
30. "Oh, give ___ home…"
31. Capone and Pacino
33. ___ land: Hollywood
34. Annoyance
35. Misdeeds
37. Give, as homework

40. "Peter, Peter, Pumpkin ___"

41. Make points

42. "Was ___ harsh?"

43. "…and threw up the ___"

45. Blind as ___

46. Jim Croce's "I ___ Name"

47. Tiny hill builders

48. Relax in the tub

49. ___-Caps (candy brand)

51. WC

Solution on Page 297

ACROSS

1. Pas' mates
4. Fitting
7. Mr. Spock's forte
12. Takes too much, briefly
13. Stephen of *The Crying Game*
14. Sports stadium
15. Monticello and Mount Vernon, e.g.
17. Tennessee footballer
18. *Delta of Venus* author Anais
19. Egypt's Mubarak
20. Examples
23. Seminary subj.
24. *Dancing with the Stars* network
25. Word form for "trillion"
28. "Do I dare to ___ peach?"
32. Speedwagon letters
33. Chat room chuckle
34. Dine
35. ___ precedent
37. Perceives
39. Washington's bill
40. Lemon meringue, for one
42. Sidewalk eateries
44. Evil spirit
47. Farm enclosure
48. Appearance
49. Detection devices
53. More friendly
54. Kit ___ bar
55. 5th month in France
56. Welcome
57. Many mos.
58. Train depot: abbr.

DOWN

1. A Stooge
2. Product pitches
3. Mach 1 breaker
4. Manet or Monet
5. Ball-shaped hammer part
6. Coll. helpers
7. Machine shop tool
8. Baltimore baseballer
9. *As Good as It* ___ (1997)
10. ___ instant (quickly)
11. "Please?"
16. *Wheel of Fortune* buy
20. Detroit products
21. Have ___ in one's bonnet
22. Kilt wearer
23. Respiratory sound
26. "What ___ can I say?"
27. Precious eggs
29. Starting on
30. Ditty
31. Tarzan's raisers
36. Orbital high point
38. Perfumes
41. Motionless

218

43. Q and A part: abbr.

44. Small dent on a fender

45. Kuwaiti leader

46. Anti-attacker spray

47. Bartlett or Bosc

49. Cloud backdrop

50. Mantra syllables

51. Lab animal

52. Break a commandment

Solution on Page 298

ACROSS

1. Sound of escaping air
5. Vicious of the Sex Pistols
8. Brazilian soccer great
12. "Not on ___!" ("No way!")
13. Tee-___
14. NYSE competitor
15. 1978 Village People hit
16. Canine cry
17. Donate
18. Receive
20. X-rated
22. Not present
25. Half a diam.
26. Merry month
27. Ruby, for one
29. West Indies republic
33. Country lodge
34. Genetic info
36. Stanley Cup org.
37. Coffee that won't keep you up
40. Peculiar
42. 3-in-1 product
43. ___ 'til you drop
45. Decorates
47. African adventure
50. Actress Ryan
51. "This won't hurt ___!"
52. Intel org.
54. Rolling in dough
58. All's opposite
59. Its symbol is Sn
60. Reverberate
61. ___-in-the-wool
62. Take your pick
63. Pass over

DOWN

1. Cow chow
2. PC maker
3. Fraction of a min.
4. Thespian's platform
5. Break into bits
6. Suffix with cloth or cash
7. Postpone
8. Chinese temple
9. Give off, as light
10. Jeans purveyor Strauss
11. Business VIP
19. Subj. including grammar
21. Word of cheer
22. In a crowd of
23. The ___ of one's existence
24. In ___ (together)
28. L–P link
30. "___ out?" (dealer's query)
31. Slender
32. Contents of Pandora's box
35. Unyielding
38. Let up

1	2	3	4		5	6	7		8	9	10	11
12					13				14			
15					16				17			
			18	19			20	21				
22	23	24					25					
26				27		28		29		30	31	32
33					34		35			36		
37			38	39		40		41		42		
			43		44		45		46			
47	48	49					50					
51					52	53			54	55	56	57
58					59				60			
61					62				63			

39. Part of FYI

41. Ike's initials

44. Mottled bean

46. Fairy-tale monsters

47. Beach composition

48. Johnny Cash's "___ Named Sue"

49. Just dandy

53. Nurse a drink

55. "That's gross!"

56. The Windy City, for short

57. Short flight

Solution on Page 298

ACROSS

1. Graph paper pattern
5. Barbell abbr.
8. *Little ___ of Horrors*
12. Weary comment
13. Hosp. scanner
14. Four years, for a US president
15. Movie unit
16. Holiday quaff
17. Sums
18. Chopped liver spread
19. Writer/illustrator Silverstein
21. Pinnacle
24. One of the simple machines
28. Hook-shaped New England
    peninsula
32. Theater school study
33. Nonwinning tic-tac-toe line
34. Quickly
36. Cashew, for one
37. Gives for a time
39. It's her party
41. Fisher or Foy
42. Co. that merged into Verizon
43. Nasdaq rival
46. Half of Mork's goodbye
50. Skywalker of Star Wars
53. Old what's-___-name
55. Gulp down
56. Letters on a phone's "0" button
57. Printer's need
58. Made for ___ other
59. Bowery bum
60. Tire pressure meas.
61. Changes the color of

DOWN

1. *The World According to ___*
2. *Cheers* actress Perlman
3. "Since ___ You Baby" (1956 hit)
4. Wipe out electronically
5. Trio before O
6. Male sibs
7. Sound of relief
8. Less fresh
9. "___ give you the shirt off his back"
10. California's Fort ___
11. Parliament VIPs
20. Most senior
22. Irish dramatist Sean
23. Break, as a balloon
25. Windmill blade
26. Grounded Australian birds
27. Sewer rodents
28. ___ slaw
29. Chopped
30. Frog's home
31. Morse code bit
35. Gear tooth
38. Pesos

40. ___ up (got nervous)

44. "Shape up or ___ out!"

45. "One," to Hans

47. "Off with you!"

48. "No more Mr. ___ Guy!"

49. Exclamations of disgust

50. Near the bottom

51. News agcy.

52. Documentary filmmaker Burns

54. Compete in a slalom

Solution on Page 298

ACROSS

1. English TV-radio inits.
4. IRS experts
8. Cold and ___ season
11. Neighbor of Vietnam
13. Ponce de ___
14. Wheel edge
15. Actress Daly
16. Paul who sang "Diana"
17. Current unit, for short
18. "No ifs, ___, or buts!"
20. Bill of Microsoft
22. Whooping ___
25. CBS forensic drama
26. Scientific workplace
27. Author Sandburg
30. Barbecue offerings
34. "___ had it up to here!"
35. Shish ___
37. Strike lightly
38. Stack
40. Stay out of sight
41. That special touch, briefly
42. Craven or Unseld
44. Enticing smell
46. "___ on a true story"
49. Verifiable
51. "Son ___ Preacher Man"
52. Swedish furniture retailer
54. Faucet sound
58. "I don't reckon so"
59. Old salts
60. Faction within a faith
61. Ambulance destinations, for short
62. Scissors cut
63. Soup legume

DOWN

1. Diner sandwich
2. Cuba's ___ of Pigs
3. Bamboozle
4. Dressed
5. Writing implements
6. Just great
7. Hosiery mishaps
8. People rush to get in here
9. Margarita ingredient
10. Baseball officials, for short
12. Connery of 007 fame
19. Narrow part of a bottle
21. Beach ball filler
22. Cut, as nails
23. Sitar player Shankar
24. Cain's brother
25. Blockhead
28. Sounds of pleasure
29. Batter's stat.
31. *Leave ___ Beaver*
32. Soothing ointment
33. Pet lovers' org.

224

36. Steady guy

39. Dolly the clone, e.g.

43. Revises, as text

45. Wines that aren't whites

46. Femur or fibula

47. "It's ___ cry from…"

48. Old sayings

49. Ms. Garr of *Mr. Mom*

50. Coarse file

53. Alternative to KS

55. House member, for short

56. Rink surface

57. "Harper Valley ___"

Solution on Page 298

ACROSS

1. The Dalai ___
5. Delivery docs, for short
8. Voice below soprano
12. Gets on in years
13. Whisper sweet nothings
14. Handyman's need
15. Ashtray item
16. Diner's bill
17. Broke ground
18. Capital of South Korea
20. Backslide
22. Big weight
24. Stimpy's partner
25. Weapons stash
29. Do-nothing
33. Speed meas.
34. Hiss accompanier
36. 72, at Pebble Beach
37. Refine, as metal
40. Hauls down to the station
43. Where Switz. is
45. Tyrannosaurus ___
46. Wasp weapon
50. Supermarket sections
54. Possesses
55. Cut the lawn
57. Didn't go on foot
58. Supreme Court count
59. "___ Believer" (Monkees tune)
60. Apple or maple
61. Classic muscle cars
62. Wee bit
63. Seal in, as a steak's juices

DOWN

1. Chemists' workshops
2. Chills and fever
3. "Take ___ your leader"
4. Shrewd
5. Tenth mo.
6. Part of an old English Christmas feast
7. Like the designated driver
8. Within reach
9. Chicago locale, with "the"
10. Tot's little piggies
11. Merrie ___ England
19. Chaney of old films
21. Floral welcome
23. Arrest
25. Pro-___ (some tourneys)
26. Tach reading
27. "___ sells seashells…"
28. Mauna ___ (brand of macadamia nuts)
30. CD forerunners
31. "___ your heart out!"
32. Monopoly quartet: abbr.
35. Bruin Bobby

38. Telescope parts

39. Harbor craft

41. Danger color

42. Puts forth, as effort

44. Send in payment

46. iTunes download

47. Silly fool

48. ___ time (quickly)

49. City in Italia

51. Oral history

52. Thought

53. Soothsayer

56. Roll of bills

Solution on Page 299

ACROSS

1. Peruvian capital
5. Elephant's org.
8. Prefix with dexterous
12. Not a dup.
13. Arafat's org.
14. Prod
15. No longer around
16. Domestic workers
18. Getting ___ years
19. Playlet
20. Part of DJIA
23. Muhammad's birthplace
27. Athletic shoe
31. Take to the sky
32. Water closet, informally
33. Personnel
36. Dutch ___ disease
37. Newspaper page for essayists
39. With one's head held high
41. Went white
43. Desire
44. Rein in
47. "Make ___!" (Picard's order)
51. Timetable
55. Scattered, as seed
56. Stratford-___-Avon
57. Buck Rogers portrayer ___ Gerard
58. Not include
59. Songwriter Bacharach
60. Coppertone no.
61. *20,000 Leagues…* captain

DOWN

1. Corporate symbol
2. Press, as clothes
3. Skimpy skirt
4. Meeting plan
5. Family MDs
6. Bullring cries
7. Sausage meat
8. Certain marbles
9. After Sun.
10. Louisville Slugger
11. Doorkeepers' demands, briefly
17. Get-up-and-go
21. Gives the go-ahead
22. Like monsoon season
24. Dorm designation
25. Summon
26. Military organization
27. Dinner from a bucket
28. California wine county
29. Stunt rider Knievel
30. Grammy category
34. Cook, as bacon
35. "Friend or ___?"
38. Not half bad
40. A choir may sing in it
42. Firecracker that fizzles

228

45. Carpets

46. Radar signal

48. Large volume

49. Triathlon leg

50. Seeing through the deception of

51. Long sandwich

52. "Brain" of a PC

53. Opposite of vert.

54. Keebler cookie maker

Solution on Page 299

ACROSS

1. Wire measure
4. Slave Scott
8. Star Trek helmsman
12. Infamous Amin
13. Winged peace symbol
14. Bloke
15. Plato's teacher
17. Heavenly music maker
18. Pooh's gloomy pal
19. Olympic sled
20. Doesn't exist
22. Walked unsteadily
24. Prosecutors, for short
25. Shoe part
28. Pub order
29. Subway coin
30. Atlas feature
33. Prayer beads
34. ___ snail's pace
35. Understood by few
38. Studio stages
39. Like a junkyard dog
40. Prickly plant
44. On a grand scale
45. Got one's bearings
48. One billionth: prefix
49. Do, re, or mi
50. *Norma* ___ (Sally Field film)
51. One who tints fabrics
52. Lambs' ma'ams
53. "…blessing ___ curse?"

DOWN

1. Prefix for giving or taking
2. "If ___ say so myself"
3. Driver's ID
4. WWII turning point
5. ___-Rooter
6. "…lived happily ___ after"
7. Military runaway
8. Carry all over the place
9. Self-mover's rental
10. The "L" of XXL
11. Raised, as an ante
16. Part of AARP: abbr.
20. Where Boise is: abbr.
21. Mineo of film
23. "___, meeny, miney, moe…"
25. Have ___ good authority
26. Rocket's forward section
27. Reggae relative
30. Eminent conductor
31. Member of the bar: abbr.
32. Mas' mates
33. Ill will
35. Revise
36. Settle, as a debt
37. *The* ___ *Mutiny*
38. "Here Comes the ___"

41. "…and pretty maids all in ___"

42. Quote as an example

43. Placekickers' props

46. Commonly pierced body part

47. Antidrug agcy.

Solution on Page 299

ACROSS

1. TLC part
5. Animal in a sty
8. Suds maker
12. Wise ___ owl
13. Goof
14. "___ Love Her"
15. Salon job
16. Friend, in France
17. Having little fat
18. Capri and Wight
20. Newsweek rival
21. Goes first
24. Take a stab at
26. Flood embankment
27. Bullring cheer
28. LAPD alert
31. Yoko of music
32. Lucy's best friend
34. Sheep sound
35. Country music cable sta.
36. CD-___ (computer insert)
37. Ring-shaped island
39. Nev. clock setting
40. Where telecommuters work
41. Regarding
44. Wascal wabbit chaser
46. The Beatles' "___ a Woman"
47. "Wanna ___?"
48. Legal rights grp.
52. Had on
53. "It's ___-win situation!"
54. Tailor's line
55. Ages and ages
56. Moo ___ gai pan
57. Egg layers

DOWN

1. Panther or puma
2. "___ was saying…"
3. Dashed
4. Complete
5. Makes well
6. *Coffee, Tea ___?*
7. Chewy part of meat
8. Like pretzels
9. "The ___ Love" (R.E.M. hit)
10. Eve's man
11. Cone-bearing tree
19. Has the helm
21. Where to drop a coin
22. Nashville's st.
23. Door-to-door cosmetics company
25. Make a connection (to)
27. Bit of resistance
28. Ending with peek or bug
29. Tree in Miami
30. Hay bundle
33. Carryall
38. Defeat soundly

232

39. Sits for a portrait

40. Response to "Are not!"

41. R.E.M.'s "It's the End of the World ___ Know It"

42. "Scat, cat!"

43. Gull-like bird

45. Johnny Carson's successor

49. So-so grade

50. PC connection

51. Vocal stumbles

Solution on Page 299

ACROSS

1. "Guilty" or "not guilty"
5. Breezy
9. Knack for comebacks
12. Iowa crop
13. Cheese with a moldy rind
14. Patient-care gp.
15. Branch offshoot
16. Coal holders
17. Hither's partner
18. ___ Monkey Trial
20. Sounds of disapproval
21. Put down
22. Day-___ paints
24. ___ Allan Poe
27. Dance class outfit
31. Public vehicle
32. Scarlett of *Gone with the Wind*
34. Completely free
35. "Lucy in the Sky with Diamonds" band
37. Tantalize
39. Lock opener
40. High degree
41. Part of a.k.a.
44. Frozen potato brand
47. Scrooge's cry
48. Jane who loved Mr. Rochester
50. Gunk
52. Univ. email ending
53. Negligee material
54. Ballerina's dress
55. Thesaurus listing: abbr.
56. Attention ___
57. Pollution that may sting the eyes

DOWN

1. Meas. of interest
2. Minimum points
3. Idle of Monty Python
4. Zambia neighbor
5. Westminster ___
6. Center of the eye
7. Old Japanese coin
8. Positive response
9. Reasons
10. "Don't worry about me"
11. A lot
19. Conditional release
20. Toddler
22. From Frankfurt: abbr.
23. Hate with a passion
24. Decline
25. Like library books, eventually
26. Fed. property manager
27. ___ Palmas, Spain
28. Elbow's locale
29. Tear
30. Insecticide banned since 1973
33. Willie Mays, the Say ___ Kid

234

1	2	3	4	■	5	6	7	8	■	9	10	11
12				■	13				■	14		
15				■	16				■	17		
■	18			19			■		20			
■	■		21			■	22	23		■	■	■
24	25	26			■	27				28	29	30
31			■	32	33			■	34			
35			36			■	37	38				
■	■	39			■	40			■	■	■	■
41	42	43		■	44				45	46	■	
47			■	48	49			■	50			51
52			■	53				■	54			
55			■	56				■	57			

36. Fight stopper, briefly

38. Formal decrees

40. Fuss over oneself

41. Lincoln and Vigoda

42. ___ Gaga

43. Avoid deliberately

44. Willy of *Free Willy*

45. Rhythm instrument

46. Part of UAW

48. Golf pro Ernie

49. "Shut yer ___!"

51. Excavated

Solution on Page 300

ACROSS

1. Father
4. Letterman's employer
7. Hide, dog-style
11. Power co.
13. Realtor's unit
14. "And giving ___, up the chimney he rose"
15. "___ arigato, Mr. Roboto"
16. Logger's tool
17. Auction actions
18. Shells out
20. ___ the day
22. Less difficult
24. Junior, to Senior
27. Frightening
30. ___ Juan (lover)
31. Prefix with light
32. Charged particles
33. Bad-mouth
34. Fine pajama material
35. *Invasion of the Body Snatchers* container
36. Lion sign
37. Like Leif Erikson
38. Stallone's nickname
39. National song
41. All clocks are set by it: abbr.
42. Medals and trophies, e.g.
46. Trig function
49. Walk-___ (clients sans appointments)
51. Theater chain founder Marcus
52. Fast-growing city near Provo
53. Use a stool
54. "___ lineman for the county" (Glen Campbell lyric)
55. Bout enders, for short
56. "___ kingdom come..."
57. *Good Will Hunting* school

DOWN

1. Bombs that don't explode
2. Upon
3. Thin coin
4. Social rank
5. Gift container
6. Hi-fis
7. ___ Ruth
8. Prefix for corn or verse
9. Reel partner
10. QB gains
12. Recluses
19. Calendar square
21. Vase
23. ___-proof (easy to operate)
24. Use a swizzle stick
25. Big-eyed birds
26. "Just do it" sloganeer
27. Nurses a drink
28. Refrigerate

29. Artist Warhol

33. Canine examiner

34. Mogadishu native

36. On the ___ (at large)

37. Just minted

40. Overly quick

41. Precious stones

43. Ramble

44. Moore of *Disclosure*

45. Whack, as a fly

46. Heavy drinker

47. Rankle

48. Keanu in *The Matrix*

50. Biomedical research org.

Solution on Page 300

ACROSS

1. Jazz job
4. Fireplace fuel
8. Con game
12. WNW's reverse
13. Black-and-white cookie
14. Fats Waller's "___ Misbehavin'"
15. Set fire to
16. Finishes first
17. Pesters persistently
18. Buffy's weapon
20. Senator Trent
22. Hosp. areas
24. Minuscule amounts
28. Flying mammals
31. Fairy-tale meanie
34. Connector to the WWW
35. *Wheel of Fortune* buy
36. Bushy hairdos
37. Tell a whopper
38. Haw's partner
39. Small pastry
40. Take orders at, as a bar
41. Perspire
43. Minivan alternative
45. Det. Sipowicz's employer
48. Mamas' mates
52. Writing tablets
55. They're soaked up at the beach
57. Give ___ shot
58. Reason to use Clearasil
59. *Garfield* dog
60. Table support
61. Greenish blue
62. Repressed, with "up"
63. ___ & Perrins (sauce brand)

DOWN

1. Hair goops
2. "What time ___?"
3. "___ move on!"
4. Farther down
5. "Either he goes ___ do!"
6. Mil. bigwig
7. Not good, but not bad
8. ___ Domingo (Caribbean capital)
9. Espionage org.
10. *The Ice Storm* director Lee
11. McKinley, Hood, et al.: abbr.
19. Bout enders, briefly
21. Neckwear
23. Upholstered couch
25. Floor covering
26. A ___ apple
27. Hurried
28. Scroogean outbursts
29. Once again
30. Domesticate
32. Doberman's warning
33. Goes bad, as fruit

238

36. ABA member: abbr.

40. New Deal org.

42. Wilderness photographer Adams

44. Unexpected sports outcome

46. Item in an actor's hand

47. Florida's Miami-___ County

49. Tablet

50. To ___ (exactly)

51. The Lord of the Rings, e.g.

52. Sajak or Boone

53. King topper

54. Genetic info carrier

56. Yang partner

Solution on Page 300

ACROSS

1. Rockers ___ Jovi
4. Woman's undergarment
8. Made, as a web
12. Major TV maker
13. Practice, as skills
14. "House" in Spain
15. "___ not my fault!"
16. Invites
17. The "A" of IRA: abbr.
18. Sum of a column
20. Like a lemon
22. Informal affirmative
24. Feudal workers
28. Puppy pickup point
31. They may pop on planes
34. Paper in lieu of payment
35. Climbing vine
36. In armed conflict
37. Fish feature
38. ___ favor ("please," in Spanish)
39. Aid
40. Disney collectibles
41. Stockholm resident
43. Disco ___ of *The Simpsons*
45. Bullets, informally
48. Archaeological find
52. Shade of blue
55. "Would ___ to you?"
57. "Gross!"
58. Cast a ballot
59. Plumber's concern
60. ___ goo gai pan
61. Amounts of money
62. Mafia bigwigs
63. Ask too many questions

DOWN

1. UK native
2. Twice tetra-
3. Cartoonist Thomas
4. Oil-bearing rock
5. ___ Angeles
6. Writing fluids
7. South-of-the-border currency
8. Frighten
9. Cal.'s ocean
10. L.A. school
11. ___ King Cole
19. Affirmative vote
21. Cold War foe, for short
23. Seeger of The Weavers
25. Abundant
26. Thwart
27. Phoenix's NBA team
28. Playful bites
29. State frankly
30. Flammable pile
32. Leatherworker's tool
33. Knocks lightly

240

36. "Um, excuse me…"
40. Pool stick
42. Copenhageners, e.g.
44. Long hikes
46. Gentle
47. Bogus butter
49. Sugar cube

50. Composer Stravinsky
51. Bok ___ (Chinese cabbage)
52. Drugstore chain
53. "___ Are My Sunshine"
54. Source of PIN money?
56. Author Fleming or McEwan

Solution on Page 300

ACROSS

1. Revolutionary Guevara
4. The "p" in "RPM"
7. Parroted
11. Grain in Cheerios
12. Chopping tools
14. Fleming hero
15. Explosive initials
16. Yahtzee pieces
17. Rainbow shapes
18. Scorches
20. ___ *Without a Cause*
22. Butterfly catcher
23. One of the Gabors
24. Venetian blind part
27. Opposite of WSW
28. "... ___ the cows come home"
31. It's part of growing up
35. Boy in a Johnny Cash song
36. Three: prefix
37. Lots
38. Ascot
39. Morse Mayday
41. Make happen
43. Argue a case
46. ___ Mall cigarettes
47. Downhill aids
49. Feb. follower
51. Sleeves cover them
52. Radial, e.g.
53. "It's the end of an ___!"
54. Cape Canaveral acronym
55. "Smoking or ___?"
56. Striped official

DOWN

1. Foldaway bed
2. Skater Brinker
3. Suffix with kitchen
4. San Diego baseballer
5. Live and breathe
6. DVR button
7. Addis ___, Ethiopia
8. Read (over)
9. Letter accompanier: abbr.
10. Dental deg.
13. Tennis star Williams
19. Opening stake
21. 12/24 and 12/31
24. Last year's jrs.
25. Lucy of *Charlie's Angels*, 2000
26. Chowed down
27. Prefix with gram or center
28. Tit for ___
29. "Where did ___ wrong?"
30. Football great Dawson
32. Singer Redding
33. Least restrained
34. Enclosure with a MS
38. Oklahoma's second-largest city

242

39. Former veep Agnew

40. Twin Mary-Kate or Ashley

41. Actress Irene of *Fame*

42. Charitable donations

44. Part of USA

45. "I double ___ you!"

46. Skillet

48. Reunion folks

50. Spitfire fliers, for short

Solution on Page 301

ACROSS

1. It's charged in physics
4. Walk-___ (small parts)
7. Cut, as wood
11. Small battery
12. Neckline shapes
14. Like 2, 4, 6, 8…
15. "And here's to you, ___ Robinson…"
16. Extra-wide shoe size
17. Pink, as a steak
18. Glass fragment
20. On one's own
22. Rds. or aves.
23. Flanders on *The Simpsons*
24. Triumphant cries
27. "___ your age!"
28. OR personnel
31. Obi-___ Kenobi
32. Apportions, with "out"
34. Fifth qtrs.
35. Article in *Der Spiegel*
36. Freud subject
37. British gun
38. Camera type, for short
39. Bean counter, for short
41. Mistreat
43. Scuttlebutt
46. "For ___ know…"
47. Play the lead
49. Univ. dorm overseers
51. Gershwin's "___ Rhythm"
52. A portion of
53. George Harrison's "All Those Years ___"
54. Go steady with
55. Spring mo.
56. Superman foe Luthor

DOWN

1. "___ a Rock": Simon & Garfunkel
2. Rowboat pair
3. Partner of Crosby and Stills
4. Out in the open
5. Essentials
6. Have a look
7. New Testament king
8. ___ *Almighty*, 2007 film
9. "___ Off to See the Wizard"
10. Compass pt. opposite SSW
13. Hand-holding, spirit-raising get-together
19. Donkey
21. David Bowie's "___ Dance"
24. Amazement
25. "Bali ___"
26. The Beach Boys' "Barbara ___"
27. Get from ___ B
28. Period
29. Rd. or hwy.
30. Tax ID

32. "Kiss my grits" TV diner
33. Exit
37. Uncle ___
38. High-end hotel option
39. Swimmer's woe
40. Less tainted
41. Pond scum component

42. Ink spot
44. Face-to-face exam
45. Explosive anger
46. Help out
48. Burnt ___ crisp
50. Chi-town team

Solution on Page 301

ACROSS

1. Cpl.'s superior
4. Barn bird
7. City known for its Heat
12. *Hannah and ___ Sisters*
13. Comic Costello
14. Initial stage
15. Way to drone
17. Horned animal with thick skin
18. Valentine's Day bouquet
19. Collect bit by bit
21. South Seas getaway
23. Nations united
26. *Revenge of the ___*
28. One-named New Age singer
29. Absorb, with "up"
32. Awaken
34. Brain scan, for short
35. Future stallion
37. Black: Fr.
39. Froggy-throated
41. Spews lava
45. Sorority members
47. "It's been ___ pleasure"
48. Shoulder wrap
50. Latvia neighbor
52. Bellhop's employer
53. Pharmaceutical giant ___ Lilly
54. "___ objections?"
55. Shoe parts
56. Med school grad
57. Columbo and Uhura: abbr.

DOWN

1. Brief
2. Birthplace of Columbus
3. Garbage
4. Senior citizen
5. Apt rhyme for "pursue"
6. Breathing organ
7. Gourmet mushroom
8. Fill the lungs
9. Foolish
10. *All the President's ___*
11. "Who am ___ argue?"
16. Opposite of "ja"
20. TV collie
22. Pressed, as clothes
24. Needle hole
25. Lose firmness
27. Hall & Oates, e.g.
29. Jr. high, e.g.
30. Hugs, in a letter
31. Appease
33. Inconsistent
36. Masonry tool
38. Currency on the Continent
40. Puts on the market
42. Word before code or colony
43. Make impure

44. Kills, as a dragon

46. Acorn, essentially

48. "Quiet down!"

49. Gardening tool

51. ___-Blo fuses

Solution on Page 301

ACROSS

1. "Whip It" rock group
5. Snead and Spade
9. West of old films
12. Actor Sharif
13. *Meet Me ___ Louis*
14. Running a fever
15. Hip-shaking dance
16. Tech. college major
17. Pop's favorite
18. Actions on heartstrings and pant legs
20. Sends out
22. Play opener
25. Airline watchdog grp.
26. Flies like an eagle
27. Fleet of warships
30. Spicy
31. *Curb Your Enthusiasm* network
32. *Mad Men* network
34. Harsh
37. Say
39. Some IHOP drinks
40. Straying
41. Valuable fur
44. Festive party
45. Mon. follower
46. Trucker with a handle
48. Bearded beasts
52. Curved path
53. Adult-to-be
54. "Assuming that's true…"
55. Jabber
56. Smart-alecky talk
57. Talon

DOWN

1. Cry from Homer Simpson
2. Flightless Aussie bird
3. Kilmer of *The Doors*
4. Rhetorician
5. Prolonged attack
6. Landers and Sothern
7. Flavor enhancer
8. Creek
9. Actress Rogers who was once married to Tom Cruise
10. Loads and loads
11. Stately shade trees
19. Young ___: tykes, in dialect
21. Barnyard bleat
22. Cinder
23. Dove or love murmurs
24. London art gallery
25. Not to
27. Pres. Lincoln
28. Spreadsheet contents
29. Revival shout
31. *48___* (Nick Nolte film)
33. PC monitor

248

35. Encyclopedia bk.

36. Throws out

37. Web address, briefly

38. Heartbreaking

40. Makes, as a salary

41. Time at a hotel

42. Surrounding glow

43. At one's ___ and call

44. Bee ___ ("Stayin' Alive" singers)

47. *Who Wants to ___ Millionaire?*

49. Pro Bowl org.

50. The Beach Boys' "Surfin' ___"

51. Mother hog

Solution on Page 301

ACROSS

1. Tadpole's parent
5. Marlene Dietrich's "___ Bin Die Fesche Lola"
8. Select
12. Kind of straits
13. Fri. preceder
14. Tennis great Arthur
15. "Dear" advice columnist
16. Close relative, for short
17. Bank's property claim
18. "Get out of here!"
20. ___ and raves
21. Challenged
24. Protrude, with "out"
25. Sharif and Bradley
26. Like Abe
29. Floor cleaner
30. Periodical, for short
31. Sty resident
33. Drunk as a skunk
36. 747, e.g.
38. Zippo
39. Atoll material
40. One more time
43. Pear variety
45. Rapper Snoop ___
46. Acorn bearer
47. Flexible, electrically
51. Unit of matter
52. Certain evergreen
53. Lion's den
54. Exercise system from India
55. Gov. Bush's state
56. Tense

DOWN

1. Rx watchdog org.
2. Chest bone
3. Crystal ball, e.g.
4. Old Faithful, for one
5. "___ long way to Tipperary"
6. IOU
7. Where spokes meet
8. Roof of the mouth
9. "Beauty ___ the eye…"
10. Guitarist Atkins
11. Griffey and Kesey
19. Long-term S&L investments
20. Baseball score
21. ___ Perignon champagne
22. "Famous" cookie guy
23. Fully attentive
24. Run for exercise
26. "If I ___ a Hammer"
27. Practice in the ring
28. *30 Rock* star Fey
30. *Braveheart* star Gibson
32. Hair goo
34. WWII cipher machine

250

35. Finish in front

36. Mac alternatives

37. Place

40. "An apple ___ keeps…"

41. "___ jail" (Monopoly directive)

42. Eager

43. Bondsman's security

44. Cajun veggie

46. Wide of the mark

48. Scoundrel

49. Use a spade

50. "When Doves ___" (Prince)

Solution on Page 302

ACROSS

1. Auto racer Yarborough
5. Magnon start
8. Letters on a radio switch
12. Suffix with psych-
13. Barnyard cackler
14. "Later," to Luigi
15. Scenic view
17. ___ von Bismarck
18. Build (on)
19. Area 51 craft, supposedly
20. Use an iron
21. Cowboy hat
23. Bowling targets
26. Sixth sense: abbr.
27. Degree held by many a CEO
30. Shop without buying
33. More spooky
35. Glimpsed
36. The Pointer Sisters' "___ So Shy"
38. Pull sharply
39. Acorn producer
42. To whom a Muslim prays
45. Jamaican liquor
46. "___ Had a Hammer"
49. Stolen stuff
50. Turbulent currents
52. Cut, as expenses
53. Holiday preceder
54. ___ care in the world
55. ___ and ends
56. Neckline shape
57. Group with a common ancestor

DOWN

1. Nightclub in a Manilow tune
2. Just ___ (not much)
3. The Swedish Nightingale
4. Environmental prefix
5. Rub raw
6. Far off
7. ___ roll (winning)
8. Oak-to-be
9. Tiny pest
10. Minnesota ___
11. Cattle calls
16. Same old grind
20. *The ___ of Greenwich Village* (1984 movie)
21. 180 degrees from NNE
22. NNW opposite
23. Viewer-supported network: abbr.
24. Money for the senior yrs.
25. Right this minute
27. Farrow of films
28. Jerry's ice cream partner
29. Noah's craft
31. Ayatollah's predecessor
32. Mouse spotter's cry
34. White or wheat alternative

252

Puzzle 122

37. Try hard

39. Singers Hall & ___

40. Indian coin

41. CPR giver

42. Dog food once hawked by Ed McMahon

43. Dumptruckful

44. The ___ of the Rings

46. Matinee hero

47. Greek cheese

48. "This ___ outrage!"

50. Minister, slangily

51. Bus. name ending

Solution on Page 302

PUZZLES • 253

ACROSS

1. "___ me?"
4. Home loan agcy.
7. ___-tac-toe
10. Radiator emanation
12. Terra firma
14. Ref's relative
15. "Lions and tigers and bears" follower
16. Prefix with potent or present
17. "Long ago and ___ away..."
18. Stow, with "away"
20. Oneness
22. Pokes around
25. Time delay
26. Took the pennant
27. Car for hire
29. Painter Matisse
33. "Sometimes you feel like ___ ..."
35. Open ___ night
37. Frog's relative
38. ___ buddies
40. Talk incessantly
42. Submachine gun
43. Tic-toe connector
45. High on something other than life
47. Jigsaw puzzle unit
49. Young bear
50. Ceiling fixture
51. ___ Romeo (Italian car)
53. Wry Bombeck
57. BPOE member
58. Unwanted lawn growth
59. Thumbs-up votes
60. Susan of *L.A. Law*
61. First-round pass
62. ___ choy (Chinese green)

DOWN

1. "___ died and made you king?"
2. Snickering syllable
3. Candied veggie
4. Jetsam's partner
5. Popular Easter dish
6. Cancel
7. Clump of hair
8. "If ___ be so bold..."
9. EMT's skill
11. Proofreader's find
13. Entertainer Shore
19. Merchandise ID
21. The Beach Boys' "___ Around"
22. Clean the deck
23. Thing you shouldn't do
24. Responsibility
28. Oversized
30. Verb accompanier
31. Level to the ground
32. "Look what ___!"
34. Shopping bag

36. Fall like Niagara's waters

39. Colorful parrot

41. A/C meas.

44. Star

46. Follow orders

47. Ashen

48. Like printers' fingers

50. Gave grub to

52. Tina of *30 Rock*

54. Dixie soldier

55. Chinese chairman

56. "___ not what your country…"

Solution on Page 302

ACROSS

1. Wedding vows
5. Anatomical pouch
8. Window box location
12. Campbell's product
13. "This ___ fine how-do-you-do!"
14. Captain Picard's counselor
15. ___ snuff (adequate)
16. Vice president Quayle
17. Glowing review
18. Mortar's partner
20. Tickles the fancy
22. Weep
23. Teapot topper
24. MD's helpers
27. Bench with a back
29. Ignited again
33. Weight-loss plan
35. Mad Hatter's drink
37. Companionless
38. Hide for future use
40. Family room
42. Lass
43. "Rumor ___ it…"
45. Head-butt
47. Slot-machine site
50. Andre of tennis
54. "___ in every garage"
55. "___ chance!"
57. Has the oars
58. Fuel from a bog
59. "Who ___ we kidding?"
60. Grand ___ home run
61. Spheres
62. Part of PST: abbr.
63. Beer ingredient

DOWN

1. "The jig ___!"
2. Simpleton
3. On the ___ (not speaking)
4. Leopard features
5. Auxiliary wager
6. Hard ___ rock
7. Panama waterway
8. German dessert
9. Gershwin and others
10. Valentine sentiment
11. Fibs
19. Cut off
21. Old space station
24. Hwys.
25. Annual coll. basketball competition
26. Adriatic or Aegean
28. "With this ring, I thee ___"
30. Nautical journal
31. Put ___ good word for
32. Business card no.
34. Items worn with shorts
36. Infused with oxygen

Puzzle 124

39. Liu Pang's dynasty
41. Over-the-hill horse
44. Couches
46. Bog
47. Mafia boss
48. Taiwanese PC maker
49. Swedish car

51. Duet minus one
52. Horse trade
53. Beliefs
56. The "A" in MoMA

Solution on Page 302

ACROSS

1. Young boy
4. Baking soda meas.
7. Wall St. debut
10. Messy type
12. Inventor's cry
13. Put in the overhead bin, say
14. Prohibit
16. Selfish one's exclamation
17. ___-do-well
18. Walking sticks
19. Jack of nursery rhyme
22. Top-___ (best)
24. Nut
25. "___ One Bites the Dust"
29. Thomas Edison's middle name
30. Terminus
31. Relinquish
32. Holy
34. Actress Lena
35. Best buds
36. Cleanser brand
37. Post of etiquette
40. Watered down
42. Anderson of *WKRP in Cincinnati*
43. Attack verbally
47. Hay storage place
48. ___ Moines
49. Web auction site
50. Big fuss
51. Place for a pig
52. Feel sick

DOWN

1. "Lucy in the Sky with Diamonds" subject, supposedly
2. Three-time Frazier foe
3. MS-___
4. *A ___ of Two Cities*
5. Pleasantly concise
6. Cat's foot
7. Pack ___ (quit)
8. Cornmeal bread
9. Has creditors
11. Dairy Queen offering
13. Clever person
15. Give permission
18. Corp. top dog
19. Hunk
20. Gallup specialty
21. Wander about
23. Ill. neighbor
26. Captain's position
27. Falco of *The Sopranos*
28. Monthly payment
30. Snakelike fish
33. "___ cheese!"
36. Auto
37. Fitzgerald of song
38. Word before ring or swing

39. Press release contents

41. Posing no challenge

43. Football scores, for short

44. Wizards and Magic org.

45. ___ chi (Chinese discipline)

46. Popeye's Olive

Solution on Page 303

ACROSS

1. Where the Styx flows
6. Fed. emissions watchdog
9. Once around a track
12. Mentally acute
13. Cup's edge
14. Satisfied sigh
15. Wyoming's Grand ___ National Park
16. Matterhorn or Mont Blanc
17. Hopping ___
18. Duo plus one
20. Large bodies of water
21. *The ___ Squad*
24. Foreword, for short
26. Gardner of *The Night of the Iguana*
27. *The Waste Land* poet's monogram
28. Largest artery in the body
32. Professor's job security
34. Temper, as metal
35. Wipe, as a blackboard
36. Kind of PC monitor
37. Scrape (by)
38. Cosmetics maker Lauder
40. Beer container
41. Pouches
44. Hinged fastener
46. Mil. entertainment group
47. Reaction to the cold
48. Songwriters' grp.
53. Recyclables container
54. Nancy Reagan's son
55. Stir up, as a fire
56. ___ Fernando Valley
57. Sit-up targets
58. Water balloon sound

DOWN

1. Stetson or sombrero
2. Go gray, maybe
3. Telegraph signal
4. "Xanadu" rock grp.
5. Shipped
6. Julia's *Seinfeld* role
7. Aviator
8. PC program
9. Weak, as an excuse
10. Tiny battery size
11. Advanced degrees
19. "All ___!" (court phrase)
20. Part of ASAP
21. "G'day" recipient
22. Eggs ___ easy
23. Delany of *China Beach*
25. ___ McNally (atlas publisher)
27. Uno plus dos
29. Really smell
30. Seize
31. Words after shake or break

260

33. Employs

34. Versatile blackjack holdings

36. Gets smart

39. Pulsate

41. Sits in (for)

42. China's continent

43. NY neighbor

45. Football throw

47. Playtex offering

49. Gas additive brand

50. KFC's Sanders, e.g.

51. Alias initials

52. Four-footed friend

Solution on Page 303

ACROSS

1. ___-Atlantic
4. Risk-free
8. What a worker earns
12. "___ the Force, Luke"
13. Happy as a ___
14. Skater's spinning leap
15. Loud noise
16. Lubricates
17. Go under
18. Backs of boats
20. Greets the day
21. "Bless you" preceder
23. Radio host Don
26. Restaurant activity
31. Italian cheese
34. Wizard of Menlo Park
35. Hung around
36. See-___ (transparent)
37. Riches
41. Banana treat
45. Most achy
48. Dry as a desert
49. Michelle Wie's org.
50. Kernel holder
52. Brubeck of jazz
53. Supply-and-demand subj.
54. Self-proclaimed psychic Geller
55. Examines closely
56. Catholic ritual
57. Small amount

DOWN

1. Kind of pie
2. Egyptian goddess
3. Fender bender result
4. Treat with contempt
5. Draw ___ in the sand
6. Not true
7. Typesetter's units
8. "Now, where ___?"
9. Line of rotation
10. Heredity unit
11. Lodge members
19. English class assignment
20. Use a book
22. Last of 26
23. E-file receiver
24. Bon ___ (clever remark)
25. Thurman of *Gattaca*
27. Church donation
28. Kind of: Suffix
29. "Neither snow ___ rain…"
30. Bearded grazer
32. Former House Speaker Gingrich
33. "___ to Billie Joe"
38. Pet welfare org.
39. Corporate symbols
40. ___ fat

262

41. Marquis de ___

42. Appeal to God

43. Not prerecorded

44. "Beware the ___ of March"

46. Gulf War missile

47. ___ Bora (Afghan region)

49. Moon vehicle

51. Baby's dinner wear

Solution on Page 303

ACROSS

1. "I'm Gonna Wash That Man Right ___ My Hair"
5. "___ Gang" comedies
8. "___ to differ"
12. ___ and cons
13. End of most work wks.
14. Basketball great Archibald
15. Hideous
16. The old soft shoe
18. Order to a broker
19. Lustful look
20. Tiny Tim played one
23. With the sound off
27. Like some cell phone charges
31. *Julius Caesar* costume
32. Breakfast staple
33. ___-garde
36. Path
37. *30 Rock* costar Baldwin
39. Leaves high and dry
41. Olympic award
43. Attila, e.g.
44. Hitchhiker's quest
47. Mil. weapon that can cross an ocean
51. Pittsburgh team
55. Beauty mark
56. ___ d'oeuvres
57. Actress Zadora
58. Ever and ___
59. Hankerings
60. ___-Mex cuisine
61. Ribald

DOWN

1. Magnum ___: great work
2. Twist the arm of
3. Bridge-crossing fee
4. Refugee's request
5. Frequently, to a bard
6. ___ Mountains: Europe/Asia border range
7. Like a yellow banana
8. Bound by routine
9. Make taboo
10. And so on: abbr.
11. "Fancy that!"
17. Rep.'s rival
21. Sedona maker
22. Letter holder: abbr.
24. Word after boom or Bean
25. "Heavens to Betsy!"
26. Calendar units
27. Paper measure
28. Leer at
29. Like mellower wines
30. Electric alternative
34. To the ___ degree (extremely)
35. *In Cold Blood* writer, to pals

38. Stroke gently

40. It's not vegetable or mineral

42. Rapper ___ Wayne

45. Govt. branch

46. Shallowest Great Lake

48. Dunce cap, geometrically

49. What winds do

50. Repair, as a tear

51. Hardly extroverted

52. It may test the waters

53. Directional suffix

54. Bill Clinton's instrument

Solution on Page 303

ACROSS

1. "Ars gratia artis" studio
4. Show showers
7. Like sushi
10. "Up and ___!"
12. Is down with something
14. Have yet to pay
15. Morse ___
16. Badly claw
17. Duck for apples
18. Mountain pass
20. Force back
22. Abrasion
25. I.M. ___
26. "Tippecanoe and Tyler ___"
27. Part of NATO: abbr.
29. ___ firma
33. Graduate, for short
35. Bro's relative
37. Thailand, once
38. Croc's cousin
40. "Uh-uh"
42. "We ___ People…"
43. Culture-supporting org.
45. Compulsion by threat
47. Like a sombrero's brim
49. "Look at Me, I'm Sandra ___"
50. "The Fall of the House of Usher" writer
51. Sup
53. Dull-colored
57. Long. opposite
58. High-protein beans
59. Bamboozle
60. Since Jan. 1, in financials
61. "Quiet on the ___!"
62. Computer program glitch

DOWN

1. ___ and cheese
2. Classic muscle car
3. ___ school
4. Monkeys (with)
5. By way of
6. Soup eater's sound
7. Boxer's pre-bout wrap
8. Missing, militarily
9. World Wide ___
11. Prefix with byte
13. Winter precipitation
19. Sgt.'s mail drop
21. Pecan and pumpkin
22. Guys-only party
23. Coke or Pepsi
24. Lopsided victory
28. Tonic's mate
30. ___ of passage
31. Arena cheers
32. Spy Aldrich
34. Pre-stereo sound

266

36. Most blue

39. Enjoys a book

41. Palette selection

44. "Hasta la vista!"

46. Actor Foxx

47. Canoe or kayak

48. No longer working: abbr.

50. Tissue paper layer

52. Bill ___ the Science Guy

54. "Ay, there's the ___"

55. Storekeeper in The Simpsons

56. Implore

Solution on Page 304

ACROSS

1. Radio's PBS
4. Letter carriers' grp.
8. Zig's opposite
11. Buzzer in a hive
12. Classic soda pop
13. Serve coffee
14. Radar gun aimer
15. Graceful bird
16. Part of the mezzanine
17. Branching-out point
19. ___ fish sandwich
21. Big galoot
23. Ab strengthener
26. Like some traits
30. Sat for a portrait
32. Mickelson's org.
33. Nevertheless
35. Wine descriptor
36. Growing older
39. On the line
42. Black-and-white cookies
44. Crow sound
45. School orgs.
47. Dark film genre
50. Peruvian native
53. Get one's dander up
55. Helpful hint
57. Blockhead
58. Many are about nothing
59. Chem. or phys.
60. Work undercover
61. Adjacent (to)
62. "Are we having fun ___?"

DOWN

1. Peacock network
2. Lowly laborer
3. ___ *Man* (Estevez film)
4. Remove from office
5. Stitch up
6. Contemporary "cool"
7. Nasal cavity
8. Animal park
9. Mo. after July
10. College sr.'s test
13. Philosopher who wrote the *Republic*
18. Bambi's mother, for one
20. ___ and tuck
22. ___ to be tied (angry)
24. Beef-rating org.
25. Job benefit
26. Dean's list fig.
27. Breakfast brand
28. Hair removal brand
29. When repeated, a Latin dance
31. Go blonde, say
34. Like some stocks: abbr.
37. Katmandu's land

38. "I ___ Rhythm"

40. Most sensible

41. "___ can play that game"

43. Brand of wrap

46. Pro or con, in a debate

48. "___ Bitsy Spider"

49. Paddy crop

50. "No ___, ands, or buts!"

51. M-Q link

52. Coquettish

54. Smoked salmon

56. Peach center

Solution on Page 304

Answers

Puzzle 1

Puzzle 2

Puzzle 3

Puzzle 4

Puzzle 5

```
R A M S   A F T   C H A N
O B O E   R U E   H O L Y
T A L L   I N A S E N S E
S T E E P S   E X E
      C A T N A P   Y E P
D I R T P O O R   B Y E
U S E   A T S E A   E E G
M A D   L E A R N E R S
P T A   R E S C U E
    L A C   O N L I N E
I T E R A T E D   S N O W
D O R M   U K E   O F N O
A M T S   B E S   N O O K
```

Puzzle 6

```
W H Y   E N V   P A C E D
P O E   M A H   E B O L A
A N T L E R S   A L I E N
    C R Y   L A N C E
P R A D A   P E Z
L I V   L Y L E   E A V E
U F O   D O O N E   M I G
M E N D   L U N A   B A G
    I C K   R A I L S
R A W E R   M A X
E V I T A   D E C L A R E
D I N E S   O S H   R U B
O D O R S   W O E   K G B
```

Puzzle 7

```
T S A   A B A   O M S
Y O N   S T U N S   P I A
P U T   T E N E T   T R I
O P E R A S   M O R S E L
    C U R T   O W E
C R E T E   I N S I D E R
A D D   R T E   E L M
T S E T S E S   S P A I N
    H T S   L A R D
A S S U R E   A L O H A S
I O U   E A G L E   E L O
D O E   P L E A S   A P R
S T Y   S E W   D S T
```

Puzzle 8

```
A N O   R E A C T   J A I
L E D   A S F O R   O U T
I D O N T C A R E   A D S
    M O T   R O M A N I A
A D E A L   N O D
L I T H E   A E R O S O L
A B E   P S T   T A U
I S R A E L I   A V E R T
    B R A   R E E S E
B A S S E T S   L I P
A T O   C E A S E L E S S
B A N   T A L O N   S T N
A N G   S U E D E   T A O
```

ANSWERS • 273

Puzzle 9

Puzzle 10

Puzzle 11

Puzzle 12

274

Puzzle 13

Puzzle 14

Puzzle 15

Puzzle 16

Puzzle 17

```
A U F . R A F . . A S T I
G P A . E R A S . D E A F
R O W . N E X T . D A L I
I N N A T E . O M E L E T
. . . C A L . R I D . . .
L Y M E . . H E X . G P S
B O P S . M O S . D O L E
J U G . H E W . . A T O Z
. . . P I T . S H Y . . .
A C C U S E . H A S S L E
P O O L . O W E R . L A X
I S M S . R I B S . I S P
G A B E . . N A H . P H O
```

Puzzle 18

```
A R I A . S A N D . O Y L
T I C S . A L O E . A V E
A P E S . B A W L . H E N
D E S I R E S . . C U S S
. . . S E R . G L O . . .
S T A T E . T E E T H E S
C O G . S P I T E . R V S
H O T S E A T . R I S E N
. . . I S M . P A N . . .
P S S T . C A T S C A N
A H A . S M O G . E L L A
D I G . T I N E . T U E S
S P A . L I E S . S E C T
```

Puzzle 19

```
B A B S . S H A W . T A D
A H A T . C O L E . A C U
A H M E . A T T A . I L K
. . A P T S . V A L U E
S P A D E . C E N . . .
A A H . P I P E . Y O W L
G A S . E D G E S . D O O
E R O S . L A S T . O R G
. . S S E . Y A R N S
S O R T A . C R E W . . .
A W E . L E I A . A C R O
S E C . S E N T . R H E A
H S T . A L E S . D E S K
```

Puzzle 20

```
I R A S . F I R . A T R A
F I N E . A P O . C H I N
S P E D . L A D . C O M A
. . A U L D . S E U S S
S T A T S . M U D . . .
A I R E D . S T E E P L E
D E T . D I N . . R A W
E S S A Y E D . D R O N E
. . R E G . D E S K S
B A S I S . D I S H . . .
O R E S . T I N . A C O W
W E R E . V A N . S I R I
L A B S . A S S . H O S S
```

Puzzle 21

Puzzle 22

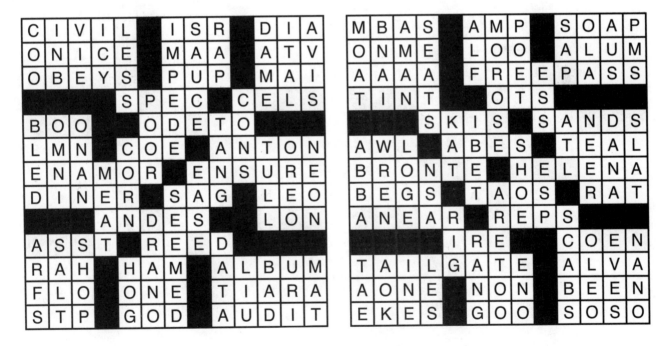

Puzzle 23

Puzzle 24

Puzzle 25

```
L A W S . C O P . B L A B
I L I E . N B A . R O S A
M I T E . N I L . A P P T
E T S Y . . E E L S . . .
. . . A E R . . E S T E R
N O B . S I F T S . O R I
T H Y . C O R E S . M I L
H O T . A T O N E . B E E
S H E E P . . D R S . . .
. . . B E D S . . L A D S
A L T S . O T C . A T E E
M A K E . L U C . P I S A
I N O N . L B S . S P I N
```

Puzzle 26

```
A W E S . C T S . . A F L
R A L E . U A W . C I A O
A D I N . M N O . A D D S
T E A S E . R E C E S S .
. . E N D . D O H . . . .
A N I S E E D . S E L E S
L E E . . N O T . . I S O
P A R S E . S E D A T E S
. . H E S . N E T . . . .
S T R E E T . S L A T S .
L O A D . A R D . A B O O
E R R S . B O A . S C O T
D I E . S O N . . T S K S
```

Puzzle 27

```
A T M . D O M . . S I N G
S O Y . E R I C . L A O S
K I N . M A C A D A M I A
S T A T E N . R U N . . .
. . . W A G . E N T R A P
S A L I N E . S E S A M E
U N O . . . . . C O N .
I N A S E C . A C C E S S
T A M A L E . T O V . . .
. . . C I D . B A S S E T
L I P R E A D E R . T Z U
O W I E . R O S S . O R B
B O N D . . G T E . W A S
```

Puzzle 28

```
S O T . S T A R . S C A B
A R I . T I R E . H A D A
L E S S E N E D . A T O N
. . . T E S T . T H E S E
C H A I R . H M O S . . .
L O S E . M A E S . P R E
A L A S K A . A S S A I L
M A N . R Y A N . P I C K
. . L I S T . T I D E S
B A B E S . T H I N . . .
A L L A . D I A M E T E R
I P O S . E L S E . A P E
T O T E . M A T S . C A N
```

278

Puzzle 29

```
C P U . O D D . . S W A P
H O P . M A I M . P E R U
A N I S E T T E . E S P N
R E N E G E . A B C . . .
. . D A D . S U S A N . .
J A D A . F L Y . M O W .
I W O N . L A Y . R O A R
M A P . K A Y . A R M Y .
. Y E S E S . K L M . . .
. . L Y E . N E P A L I .
F U M E . R H E O S T A T
I Z O D . S E E N . T V S
L I D S . . F L A . Y A Y
```

Puzzle 30

```
P A N E . E R S . . K I D
I D O S . D A H . S I N O
P I N T . A G A . A T M E
S M E A R S . R I N S E S
. . T O N . P V T . . . .
D E L E T E S . S A L E M
I P O . R A M . . I I I .
P I T A S . C A R E E N S
. . R U M . L E N . . . .
C A B A N A . A V A I L S
A D A B . S O I . C H A T
S E T S . O W S . T O M E
H E H . N N E . S P E W
```

Puzzle 31

```
G A Y . B A R E . H A D
O P U S . O R A L . E C O
B A L E . G R I D . S H A
S T E N T . E N E M I E S
. . S U E S . R E T . . .
F C C . N A T S . M A S T
E R A S E R . A D O N I S
W O R E . L A N A . T R E
. . N E V . D E W S . . .
A M E R I C A . N A S A L
T A G . L O G O . S E T A
I T I . L O I N . S L O T
T H E . A P O S . F E E
```

Puzzle 32

```
T I M . A B B R . P R O D
S T U . L I L O . A K I N
P C S . A C A T . C O L A
S H E E N . H E R E . . .
. . U S B . A R C E D
B O A R . R O L Y . O V O
Y R S . G A P E S . V A C
E B W . A S T O . M E S S
S E E D Y . N A G . . .
. . R E A L . S M A S H
L P G A . J O G S . C H A
S O A K . A N I N . D O N
U R G E . R E G S . C O D
```

Puzzle 33

Puzzle 34

Puzzle 35

Puzzle 36

Puzzle 37

Puzzle 38

Puzzle 39

Puzzle 40

Puzzle 41

Puzzle 42

Puzzle 43

Puzzle 44

Puzzle 45

Puzzle 46

Puzzle 47

Puzzle 48

Puzzle 49

Puzzle 50

Puzzle 51

Puzzle 52

Puzzle 53

Puzzle 54

Puzzle 55

Puzzle 56

Puzzle 57

Puzzle 58

Puzzle 59

Puzzle 60

286

Puzzle 61

```
P A D . . C A D . . . A D J
G O A T . R C A . W W I I .
A L M A N A C S . H O N G .
. . K I W I . M E L T S . .
I M P E L . D E A R . . . .
N E A T . . E S S E N C E .
L E C H . S N L . S O U L .
A T T E M P T . . W I R E .
. . C A R P . H A R E M . .
A T P A R . R E E L . . . .
L O O K . T O A N D F R O .
B O R E . A N S . O L I N .
A L T . . B E T . . . A P T
```

Puzzle 62

```
U P C . . T I C . . . M U D
G L O B . E D U . F O R A .
H O L O G R A M . R O L L .
. . X I I . . . . M E S S Y
A N G E L . B I R D . . . .
B E A R . . A S I A G O . .
S U M S . B R R . S U N S .
. T E H R A N . . T R I G .
. . O O H S . T A U N T . .
S H I R T . . C H I . . . .
L E F T . A D H E R E T O .
O A F S . L I E . E N V Y .
P L Y . . P E W . . . D S L
```

Puzzle 63

```
R U B S . L A M . . I S O F
S T O P . T R Y . D O O R .
V A N E . D O T . A W H O .
P H E W . U H U H . . . . .
. . S I G N . N O D E S . .
G P S . N E D . L A R V A .
R E N A M E . V E N E E R .
A N I T A . S I S . I L K .
S T P A T . M E S A . . . .
. . L E G O . . . S H O W .
E C H O . L O B . T U N A .
L U I S . O T C . A L L Y .
K E D S . P H D . B U Y S .
```

Puzzle 64

```
I D O . . F A V A . . R U M
N A B S . A P E G . I P O .
C R I T . D I A N . G A P .
A N T E S . E L E V A T E .
. . M A S C . W I T . . . .
P C T . K E E P . B O R G .
A R O U S E . E V E N S O .
L O R D . K A N E . I T D .
. . T O S . T H E N . . . .
E M I N E N T . S U M A C .
C E L . L O U D . M A T A .
O I L . M E N U . B R U T .
N R A . A L E G . C B S .
```

Puzzle 65

Puzzle 66

Puzzle 67

Puzzle 68

Puzzle 69

P	A	M		A	F	E	W		E	D	G	Y
A	S	A		G	O	N	E		M	I	R	O
H	I	C		L	O	M	B		B	O	O	K
		A	N	O	D	E		V	E	R	G	E
T	H	R	O	W		S	K	I	D			
K	I	E	V		W	H	O	S		T	I	L
O	R	N	A	T	E		C	A	N	A	D	A
S	E	A		W	A	S	H		O	P	E	C
		D	I	R	T		P	O	E	S	Y	
I	N	S	E	T		E	D	E	N	S		
D	A	L	E		B	R	I	T		T	I	N
I	P	O	D		B	E	A	T		R	B	I
G	A	B	S		C	O	Z	Y		Y	E	P

Puzzle 70

I	R	K		I	T	O		B	L	T	S
D	O	I		M	O	S	S		L	E	E	K
O	W	L		P	O	U	T		A	D	A	Y
L	E	T	H	A	L		O	M	S		
	E	L	S		N	E	E	D	L	E
C	L	A	R	A		D	E	W		Y	E	A
O	U	R	S		O	J	S		B	E	S	S
R	K	O		M	R	S		T	A	S	T	Y
D	E	N	O	T	E		G	E	M		
	M	S	G		H	E	A	R	S	T
B	I	B	I		O	F	A	N		O	L	E
A	C	U	T		N	U	N	S		M	I	R
G	U	T	S		N	A	Y		A	T	M

Puzzle 71

C	B	E	R		L	O	T		E	G	O	S
H	A	V	E		A	R	E		D	E	P	T
U	S	E	S		P	B	S		I	T	T	Y
M	E	R	E		S	H	O	T			
	T	A	N		R	O	L	E	X
T	O	P	S	E	E	D		D	R	I	V	E
A	V	A		R	E	V	U	E		E	I	N
M	A	G	M	A		D	R	A	C	U	L	A
P	L	E	A	T		I	L	L		
	S	E	C	S		A	L	I	G
C	O	A	T		T	A	R		S	I	T	E
I	D	B	E		R	A	D		S	K	I	M
D	E	E	R		L	B	S		Y	E	N	S

Puzzle 72

L	T	S		B	E	E	S		L	O	A	N
A	A	H		A	X	L	E		O	H	N	O
G	T	E		R	A	F	T		S	M	U	T
S	E	L	D	O	M		F	I	E	S	T	A
	O	N	S		R	A	S			
S	P	A	T		L	E	N		S	I	B
T	E	N	S		F	O	E		D	I	N	O
S	A	O		B	A	N		A	P	S	O
	S	I	R		S	T	N		
C	A	P	O	T	E		A	S	S	I	S	I
A	C	E	R		A	L	T	A		B	A	T
B	I	L	E		S	O	U	R		I	K	E
O	D	E	S		T	O	P	S		D	E	M

Puzzle 73

Puzzle 74

Puzzle 75

Puzzle 76

290

Puzzle 77

Puzzle 78

Puzzle 79

Puzzle 80

Puzzle 81

Puzzle 82

Puzzle 83

Puzzle 84

Puzzle 85

Puzzle 86

Puzzle 87

Puzzle 88

Puzzle 89

Puzzle 90

Puzzle 91

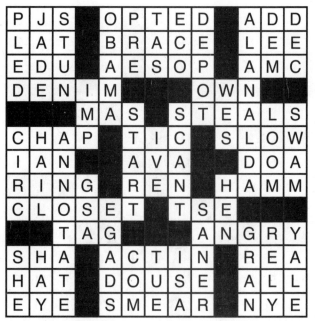

Puzzle 92

294

Puzzle 93

```
F I N D   E L K   D E P P
O P I E   V I E   A L A I
O O P S   I V Y   N E S T
      I S L E   D U E T S
N I T R O   F L U B
A C H E S   R E H E A T S
M A I     H E X   B I C
E N S N A R E   S A U N A
      I M S O   E N T E R
A L L E Y   R Y A N
B R A C   F D A   A M P S
L O D E   L I P   L E I A
E N D S   Y E S   S L A P
```

Puzzle 94

```
D J S   A B C S   M A T
N A I L   R A N T   U M S
A N D A   A T N O   T I P
      T U T   O W E N S
A S P E R   A I D E
C H I   S A T S   T O R I
T O P   A I R E S   S U B
S T E W   M E E T   H E M
      E A S E   A M A S S
R A C E D   M B A
I S H   A B B A   A R F S
G T O   M E A L   M U L E
S I P   S T Y E   N A W
```

Puzzle 95

```
S P A M   A C M E   T W A
T O D O   R O I L   Y A P
A L E S   S L A V   P I T
N E S T L E   T E N E T S
      U N E A S E
S C H   G I L   W H I P
A P O P   C U B   S I R E
M U G S   D A S   S K I
      A L I E N S
A B A T E S   S W E D E N
R O D   E T C H   M O R E
U Z I   C O V E   M E R E
N O N   H O S E   A S S T
```

Puzzle 96

```
T A P S   W H O   O N L Y
A S A P   H E F   P E T A
O K I E   Y A M   E D D Y
S A L E   R E I N
      D E F T   A S I A N
N O R   S I S   G E N R E
O P I A T E   T R A D E R
M A P L E   D U E   O A F
E L S I E   E X E S
      A M A N   C A S T
T W O S   B I G   A L L A
O O Z E   C R Y   R O A R
M O S S   D O M   S E G A
```

Puzzle 97

Puzzle 98

Puzzle 99

Puzzle 100

296

Puzzle 101

Puzzle 102

Puzzle 103

Puzzle 104

Puzzle 105

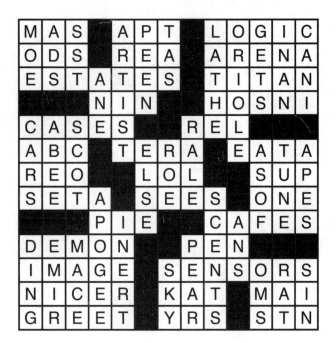

```
M A S . A P T . L O G I C
O D S . R E A . A R E N A
E S T A T E S . T I T A N
. . N I N . H O S N I
C A S E S . R E L . .
A B C . T E R A . E A T A
R E O . L O L . . S U P
S E T A . S E E S . O N E
. . P I E . C A F E S
D E M O N . P E N . .
I M A G E . S E N S O R S
N I C E R . K A T . M A I
G R E E T . Y R S . S T N
```

Puzzle 105

Puzzle 106

```
H I S S . S I D . P E L E
A B E T . H E E . A M E X
Y M C A . A R F . G I V E
. G E T . E R O T I C
A B S E N T . R A D . .
M A Y . G E M . H A I T I
I N N . R N A . . N H L
D E C A F . O D D . O I L
. B O P . A D O R N S
S A F A R I . M E G . .
A B I T . N S A . R I C H
N O N E . T I N . E C H O
D Y E D . O P T . S K I P
```

Puzzle 106

Puzzle 107

```
G R I D . L B S . S H O P
A H M E . M R I . T E R M
R E E L . N O G . A D D S
P A T E . S H E L . .
. T O P . L E V E R
C A P E C O D . D R A M A
O X O . A P A C E . N U T
L E N D S . H O S T E S S
E D D I E . G T E . .
. N Y S E . N A N U
L U K E . H I S . S W I G
O P E R . I N K . E A C H
W I N O . P S I . D Y E S
```

Puzzle 107

Puzzle 108

```
B B C . C P A S . F L U
L A O S . L E O N . R I M
T Y N E . A N K A . A M P
. A N D S . G A T E S
C R A N E . C S I . .
L A B . C A R L . R I B S
I V E . K A B O B . T A P
P I L E . H I D E . T L C
. W E S . A R O M A
B A S E D . T R U E . .
O F A . I K E A . D R I P
N A W . T A R S . S E C T
E R S . S N I P . P E A
```

Puzzle 108

Puzzle 109

Puzzle 110

Puzzle 111

Puzzle 112

Puzzle 113

```
P L E A . A I R Y . W I T .
C O R N . B R I E . H M O .
T W I G . B I N S . Y O N .
. S C O P E S . T S K S .
. . L A Y . G L O . . . .
E D G A R . L E O T A R D .
B U S . O H A R A . R I D .
B E A T L E S . T E M P T .
. . K E Y . P H D . . . .
A L S O . . O R E I D A .
B A H . E Y R E . C R U D .
E D U . L A C E . T U T U .
S Y N . S P A N . S M O G .
```

Puzzle 114

```
D A D . C B S . B U R Y
U T I L . L O T . A N O D
D O M O . A X E . B I D S
S P E N D S . R U E . . .
. . E A S I E R . S O N
S C A R Y . D O N . T W I
I O N S . D I S . S I L K
P O D . L E O . N O R S E
S L Y . A N T H E M . . .
. . G M T . A W A R D S
S I N E . I N S . L O E W
O R E M . S I T . I A M A
T K O S . T H Y . M I T
```

Puzzle 115

```
G I G . L O G S . S C A M
E S E . O R E O . A I N T
L I T . W I N S . N A G S
S T A K E . L O T T . . .
. . O R S . I O T A S
B A T S . O G R E . I S P
A N A . A F R O S . L I E
H E M . T A R T . T E N D
S W E A T . S U V . . .
. . N Y P D . P A P A S
P A D S . R A Y S . I T A
A C N E . O D I E . L E G
T E A L . P E N T . L E A
```

Puzzle 116

```
B O N . S L I P . S P U N
R C A . H O N E . C A S A
I T S . A S K S . A C C T
T O T A L . S O U R . . .
. . Y E P . S E R F S
N A P E . E A R S . I O U
I V Y . A T W A R . F I N
P O R . H E L P . C E L S
S W E D E . S T U . . .
. . A M M O . R E L I C
C Y A N . I L I E . U G H
V O T E . L E A K . M O O
S U M S . D O N S . P R Y
```

300

Puzzle 117

Puzzle 118

Puzzle 119

Puzzle 120

Puzzle 121

Puzzle 122

Puzzle 123

Puzzle 124

302

Puzzle 125

```
L A D   . T S P . . I P O
S L O B . A H A . S T O W
D I S A L L O W . M I N E
. . N E E R . C A N E S .
S P R A T . T I E R . .
L O O N . . A N O T H E R
A L V A . E N D . C E D E
B L E S S E D . O L I N .
. P A L S . C O M E T
E M I L Y . W E A K .
L O N I . T E A R I N T O
L O F T . D E S . E B A Y
A D O . S T Y . A I L
```

Puzzle 125

Puzzle 126

```
H A D E S . E P A . L A P
A G I L E . L I P . A A H
T E T O N . A L P . M A D
. . T R I O . S E A S
M O D . I N T R O . .
A V A . T S E . A O R T A
T E N U R E . A N N E A L
E R A S E . L C D . E K E
. E S T E E . K E G
S A C S . H A S P .
U S O . B R R . A S C A P
B I N . R O N . S T O K E
S A N . A B S . S P L A T
```

Puzzle 126

Puzzle 127

```
M I D . S A F E . W A G E
U S E . C L A M . A X E L
D I N . O I L S . S I N K
S T E R N S . R I S E S
S N E E Z E
I M U S . E A T I N G
R O M A N O . E D I S O N
S T A Y E D . T H R U
W E A L T H
S P L I T . S O R E S T
A R I D . L P G A . C O B
D A V E . E C O N . U R I
E Y E S . M A S S . D A B
```

Puzzle 127

Puzzle 128

```
O U T A . O U R . I B E G
P R O S . F R I . N A T E
U G L Y . T A P D A N C E
S E L L . L E E R .
U K E . M U T E D
R O A M I N G . T O G A
E G G . A V A N T . W A Y
A L E C . S T R A N D S
M E D A L . H U N .
R I D E . I C B M
S T E E L E R S . M O L E
H O R S . P I A . A N O N
Y E N S . T E X . L E W D
```

Puzzle 128

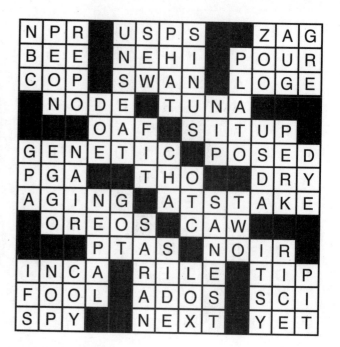

Puzzle 129

Puzzle 130